T0212091

Lecture Notes in Computer Science

Lecture Notes in Computer Science

Edited by G. Goos and J. Hartmanis

327

Gary A. Ford (Ed.)

Software Engineering Education

SEI Conference 1988
Fairfax, Virginia, USA, April 28–29, 1988
Proceedings

Springer-Verlag

New York Berlin Heidelberg London Paris Tokyo

Editor

Gary A. Ford
Software Engineering Institute, Carnegie Mellon University
Pittsburgh, PA 15213, USA

Carnegie-Mellon University
Software Engineering Institute

CR Subject Classification (1987): D.2, K.3.2

ISBN 0-387-96854-7 Springer-Verlag New York Berlin Heidelberg
ISBN 3-540-96854-7 Springer-Verlag Berlin Heidelberg New York

© Springer-Verlag Berlin Heidelberg 1988
Printed in Germany

Printing and binding: Druckhaus Beltz, Hemsbach/Bergstr.
2848/3140-543210

Preface

The Software Engineering Institute (SEI) is a federally funded research and development center operated by Carnegie-Mellon University. Its principal responsibility is to accelerate the reduction to practice of modern software engineering techniques and methods. Included in this responsibility are the identification, assessment, development, dissemination, and insertion of promising methods, techniques, and tools to support software engineering.

Recognizing that education is the foundation for substantial improvements in developing and using technology, the SEI charter also includes the sentence, "[The SEI] shall also influence software engineering curricula development throughout the education community." Our experiences to date indicate that the education community is very interested in software engineering education, and that the SEI can play an important role in focusing activities in the development of courses and curricula, in catalyzing the production of textbooks, educational software, and other course support materials, and in providing for widespread distribution of information and materials.

An annual activity of the SEI is the *SEI Conference on Software Engineering Education*. The purpose of the conference is to promote enhanced software engineering education in the academic, industrial, and government educational communities, and to promote interactions among educators in these three communities. The conference includes refereed papers, panel discussions, reports and demonstrations from the SEI; future conferences will also include exhibits and demonstrations of educational materials and software tools.

The Program Committee for the 1988 conference was:

Jon Bentley, *AT&T Bell Labs*
James Collofello, *Arizona State University*
H. E. Dunsmore, *Purdue University*
Richard Fairley, *George Mason University*
Jeffrey A. Lasky, *Rochester Institute of Technology*
H. Dieter Rombach, *University of Maryland*
Gail Sailer, *Boeing Computer Services*
James E. Tomayko, *The Wichita State University*

and, from the SEI:

Mark Ardis
Lionel Deimel
Charles Engle
Gary Ford
Norman Gibbs
Robert Glass
Harvey Hallman
Scott Stevens

Gary Ford

Pittsburgh, Pennsylvania
April, 1988

Contents

Teaching the Tricks of the Trade

Jon Bentley
AT&T Bell Laboratories
Murray Hill, NJ 07974

Introduction

Here's a trick of the medical trade useful for anyone who donates blood. Before sticking the big needle in your arm, the nurse first pricks your finger for a few drops of blood. Some thoughtless nurses jab the pad of the index finger, which is the most sensitive spot of the most used finger. It is better to poke a less sensitive part (on the side, halfway down from nail to pad) of a less commonly used finger (the ring finger). Insist on it the next time you donate blood.

Medicine has a firm basis in science: chemistry gives great insight into pharmacology and biology is essential for surgery. Techniques of project management are also obvious: surgical teams allow a dozen hands to work under one mind, and medical records are often exemplary documentation. But science and management aren't enough; excellent practitioners must also master some tricks of the trade.

The same holds true in our field. All software engineers must be familiar with relevant subdisciplines of computer science and with techniques of project management. But there is more than science and management inside the heads of excellent software engineers. They know the tricks of their trade.

By the term "Tricks of the Trade" I explicitly exclude subjects that might fall under the titles of computer science, project management, or programming techniques. Rather, I wish to emphasize what might be called "common-sense engineering". I have written about such topics in several of my "Programming Pearls" columns in *Communications of the ACM*.† This paper is about teaching these tricks in software engineering classes. We'll begin by studying one trick in detail, and then survey several others.

---

† Columns that are specifically devoted to tricks include Cracking the Oyster (August 1983), The Back of the Envelope (March 1984), Graphic Output (June 1984), Tricks of the Trade (February 1985), Bumper-Sticker Computer Science (September 1985), Cutting the Gordian Knot (February 1986), and The Envelope is Back (March 1986). Tricks are used in many of the other columns; see the index entry "engineering techniques" in the collections Bentley [1986, 1988].

Debugging

After we observe weird behavior in a software system, how do we identify the culprit that is causing the problem? That skill is often crucial in building and maintaining a software system, yet is rarely taught in books or classes. It deserves to be taught, but how should we teach it?

Stories can help a lot. In the late 1950's, Vic Vyssotsky was called to repair a program that was raising havoc at Bell Labs. On typical runs, the program worked correctly about half the time. But whenever the programmers came into the machine room, the program always worked — and because they could never see it fail, they couldn't make any progress in fixing it.

That was the only clue Vyssotsky had: the program worked whenever the programmers were present. Something apparently *knew* that the programmers were in the room. What could it be? His colleagues generated all sorts of wild theories: did the excess weight on the machine room floor cause it to sag and stretch a cable? Such conjectures are hard to test. Vyssotsky agreed that something did know that the programmers were present, and set out to find an elegant answer. Think hard about the problem for a minute: what was in the machine room that just *had* to know that the programmers were also there?

People, that's what. The computer operators could see that the programmers were in the room. With that insight, Vyssotsky was able to observe their behavior unobtrusively. When programmers were present, the operators laboriously followed official policy: mount each tape, check that it is aligned, and carefully hit the rewind button to position it properly. When they weren't being observed, though, the overworked operators would sometimes hurriedly slap the tape on the drive and let the program do the job with a software rewind command. And that led Vyssotsky to the bug in the program: the rewind instruction in that particular program had been erased (by a distant and particularly nasty bug).

There's a moral in the story. The expert debugger never forgets that there has to be a logical explanation, no matter how mysterious the behavior may seem at the time. Vyssotsky observed that something had to know that the programmers were in the room, and he conjectured the simplest possible something (which turned out to be a someone) who could know. When your software exhibits weird behavior, think hard to find a simple explanation.

There are lots of great debugging stories. When I asked Bob Martin of Bell Communications Research about the neatest bug he had ever tracked down, he responded immediately with the story of "the program that worked once twice". He watched a huge system undergoing its first field tests. When the system was booted, it correctly handled one type of query and then reported a string of errors. When the system was rebooted (for an unrelated reason) Martin observed the same behavior again: the first answer was correct, and all subsequent answers gave errors. The program worked once, twice. This was enough of a clue for Martin to tell the programmers where to find the bug: the re-initialization code was leaving a data structure in an inconsistent state.

A good debugging story now and then can be useful and fun for a software engineering class. They can usually be told in just a few minutes, and a zippy story with a good moral makes that a memorable and worthwhile investment of class time. Section 5.7 of Bentley [1988] contains a couple more stories. But homemade stories are always more exciting to tell and to hear than storebought ones; collect your own and share them with your colleagues.

In Bentley and Dallen [1987], John Dallen and I describe a software engineering course that we co-taught at the United States Military Academy. We felt strongly that we should teach debugging in the course, and scattered software stories like those above throughout the course (never more than one a week). Dallen told several fascinating debugging stories from his experiences as a military engineer; each had a moral that applies equally well to building bunkers or buffers.

We also assigned each cadet to read an essay in the best book I have ever seen on debugging: Berton Roueché's *Medical Detectives* (Roueché [1982]; a second volume has since appeared as Roueché [1986]). The heroes in the books debug complex systems, ranging from mildly sick people to very sick towns. We would then fill up those awkward five-minute holes at the end of a class by calling on a cadet to present an essay (each cadet was assigned a different essay). The cadet would then summarize the story and explain how the problem-solving methods used by the medical heroes are applicable to debugging computer systems. The students made a number of interesting analogies and had a lot of fun doing so (several cadets reported that they read the entire book — Roueché's true stories are as spellbinding as any fiction).

Computer science has a lot to say about debugging: there are elegant and useful theories of test data selection and of test coverage analysis. Software managers can use quality control techniques to analyze data on software faults. Both of those topics are taught in software engineering curricula. Tracing the manifestation of a bug to a place in a program, however, remains a trick of the trade. It's not science, it's not engineering, but it can and should be taught — gently — in software engineering classes.

Proverbs for Programmers

"Better to remain silent and be thought a fool than to speak up and remove all doubt." Even so, I'm going to offer my opinion on aphorisms: people love them. A pithy quote can be easy to remember and sometimes even useful.

Other disciplines proudly summarize the tricks of their trades in lists of adages. Strunk and White's [1979] maxims teach us about writing English:

> Revise and rewrite.
> Choose a suitable design and hold to it.
> Omit needless words.

Many of Polya's [1945] hints for mathematics are directly relevant to programming:

> Draw a figure. Introduce suitable notation.
> Look at the unknown!
> Can you derive the result differently?

Cleveland [1985, Section 2.6] presents rules for graphical displays of data.

There are many sources of aphorisms for software engineering. Kernighan and Plauger [1978] list rules for programming:

> Use the "telephone test" for readability.
> Each module should do one thing well.
> Keep it simple to make it faster.

Brooks [1975] contains a number of pithy sayings about large software projects:

> Adding manpower to a late software project makes it later.
> Plan to throw one away; you will, anyhow.
> The cost of maintaining a widely used program is typically 40 percent or more of the cost of developing it.

Lampson's [1984] "hints" are summarized in memorable slogans:

> Handle normal and worst cases separately.
> In allocating resources, strive to avoid disaster rather than to attain an optimum.

Column 6 of Bentley [1988] is titled "Bumper Sticker Computer Science"; it contains about eighty sayings like these:

> In non-I/O-bound programs, less than four percent of a program generally accounts for more than half of its running time.
> Whenever possible, steal code.
> I'd rather write programs to write programs than write programs.

Part I of Polya [1945] describes in detail how such rules can be used in a classroom. Solving software problems, like solving mathematical problems, is a practical skill that is acquired by imitation and practice. The teacher might therefore discuss the rules explicitly in small parts of a lecture or two, but the student learns them only as they are applied in solving interesting problems. The teacher should unobtrusively help the student not too much and not too little, always asking questions that might have occurred to the student himself.

Problem Definition

After 16 years of school, the average college senior has the mistaken notion that all problems come neatly packaged. Of the many wounds inflicted by modern education, this is one of the most tragic: preschool children come up with wonderfully creative solutions to problems, while graduates seem to have acquired tunnel vision.

Because I have a Ph.D. in Computer Science, I suffer from this problem most acutely. Sections 5.1 and 5.2 of Bentley [1988] describe how my problem reared its ugly head when a public opinion polling firm asked me to write a program to produce random samples from a printed list of precincts. I made the dreadful mistake of solving the problem they asked me to solve: I wrote a program. When I described the problem at West Point, a cadet observed that it was even simpler to solve a more basic problem: drawing a random sample. The cadet suggested photocopying the precinct list, cutting the copy into pieces of equal size, shaking the slips in a large paper bag, and then selecting the sample by pulling slips out of the bag.

My education left me with a conceptual block common to programmers: I tend not to see elegant solutions that don't use computers. Adams [1979] defines conceptual blocks as "mental walls that block the problem-solver from correctly perceiving a problem or conceiving its solution". His book on "conceptual block-busting" studies methods for breaking through blocks and is generally a pleasant prod towards more creative thinking. Although it was not written with programmers in mind, many of its lessons are particularly appropriate for programming problems.

One problem with such books is that so much general problem solving divorced from any particular technical area begins to look like "just puzzles". I tried to remedy that in Bentley [1986, 1988]. The columns interweave programming details with stories of finding the easy way out of some important, hard problems. Column 1 of Bentley [1986] is a case study in problem definition; see also the index entries for common sense, conceptual blocks, elegance, engineering techniques, insight, Inventor's Paradox, problem definition, and simplicity. Column 5 of Bentley [1988] is titled "Cutting the Gordian Knot"; it is about finding clever solutions to complex problems, with a heavy emphasis on solving the right problem.

Back-of-the-Envelope Calculations

A programmer is building a new system for a college data processing organization. One module in the current design does a disk access in a large database for each class taken by each student. Fortunately, the programmer knows a trick of the trade and decides to ask a relevant question: will that process take "too much" time?

The answer, of course, depends on several particulars. How much time is a disk access? A typical disk rotates at 3600 RPM, or 60 revolutions per second, or 17 milliseconds per revolution; the access time might vary from half that on the average, if we're lucky, to several times that when long seeks are involved. But let's take a middle ground, and assume 20 milliseconds per access. If 2000 students in a small college each take about 5 classes, the 10000 accesses will take about 200 seconds or 3.3 minutes, which won't be noticed if the job is run once a semester. If 40000 students at a huge state university have the same course load, though, then the task will take over an hour, and will therefore be quite unacceptable for an interactive program.

Column 6 of Bentley [1986] and Column 7 of Bentley [1988] introduce back-of-the-envelope calculations and their applications in software design. These calculations aren't second nature. In his excellent introduction to the subject, Hofstadter [1982] tells how he asked students in a New York City physics class the height of the Empire State Building, which they could see out the window. The true height is 1250 feet, but answers ranged from 50 feet to one mile. I had a similar experience in a class *after* I had given a brief lecture on "back-of-the-envelope" calculations and illustrated the calculations throughout the class. An examination question asked for the cost of a one-semester, fifteen-student class section at that college. Most students gave an answer within thirty percent of my estimate of $30,000, but the extremes ranged from a high of $100,000,000 to a low of $38.05.

Spare ten minutes of lecture for this topic, then reinforce it with little examples throughout the class. Test your success by an examination question; I bet you'll find the answers interesting.

A Sampler of Tricks

I recently attended (as an observer) a meeting of accomplished young software architects. When we discussed their educational backgrounds, it came out that every one of the dozen or so architects in the room had an engineering degree (electrical, mechanical or aeronautical; no software engineers). The architects didn't realize that they shared this educational background, but they weren't surprised to learn it. They acknowledged that their particular subjects of engineering were pretty much irrelevant to their current jobs, but they felt that they had learned "how to think like an engineer". Here are some of those thought patterns that we can encourage in software engineering classes.

Monitoring Tools. It's hard to imagine a physician without a stethoscope or an electrical engineer without an oscilloscope — they know that they must monitor objects before they manipulate them. Column 1 of Bentley [1988] describes how profilers can perform a similar role for software.

Let's Look at the Data. If you're going to build a software system for processing VLSI designs, you should first gather data on the designs: what are the typical sizes, shapes, and placements of the geometric components? Only with such data can tradeoffs be made sensibly. And whether the data you have gathered regards a problem domain or the productivity of a software organization, it can be presented more clearly using the graphical techniques of Tufte [1983], Cleveland [1985], or Column 11 of Bentley [1988].

Build with Components. Recent advances in software technology allow us to build interesting software systems by assembling software components. The components themselves vary from database systems to window packages to software pipes to subroutine libraries. Asking a software engineering class to build a software system out of lines of Pascal code is like asking an electrical engineering class to build a radio starting with a mound of sand.

Prototypes. Most engineers spend their educational years building artifacts that are (at most) prototypes; it is second nature for them to test a design on a breadboard before casting it into silicon. Software components make it easier to build software prototypes; they also give experience in building software scaffolding. Bentley and Dallen [1987] describe a software design course that depends heavily on prototyping.

Conclusions

There are many tricks of the software trade; this paper has sampled just a few. The science and management techniques underlying software are essential to any career in software engineering, but these tricks are sometimes useful. Careful use of the tricks has catapulted more than one competent young programmer into software superstardom.

I don't think that these tricks should be given a one-hour lecture in a software engineering course. Some might deserve a ten-minute lecture here or a five-minute story there. But for the most part, tricks are learned through osmosis: your students will learn them as you apply them in lectures and as your teaching assistants apply them in software laboratories. And if they do learn these tricks, both your students and their employers will be grateful to you.

References

Adams, J. L. [1979]. *Conceptual Blockbusting*, Second Edition, Norton.

Bentley, J. L. [1986]. *Programming Pearls*, Addison-Wesley, Reading, MA.

Bentley, J. L. [1988]. *More Programming Pearls: Confessions of a Coder*, Addison-Wesley, Reading, MA.

Bentley, J. L. and J. A. Dallen, Jr. [1987]. "Exercises in software design", *IEEE Transactions on Software Engineering*, November 1987.

Brooks, Jr., F. P. [1975]. *The Mythical Man-Month*, Addison-Wesley, Reading, MA.

Cleveland, W. S. [1985]. *The Elements of Graphing Data*, Wadsworth, Monterey, CA.

Hofstadter, D. [1982]. "Number numbness, or why innumeracy may be just as dangerous as illiteracy", *Scientific American*, May 1982. (Reprinted in Hofstadter's *Metamagical Themas*, Basic Books, 1985.)

Kernighan, B. W. and P. J. Plauger [1978]. *The Elements of Programming Style*, Second Edition, McGraw-Hill, New York, NY.

Lampson, B. W. [1984]. "Hints for computer system design", *IEEE Software 1*, 1, January 1984.

Polya, G. [1945]. *How to Solve It*, Princeton University Press, Princeton, NJ.

Roueché, B. [1982]. *The Medical Detectives*, Washington Square Press.

Roueché, B. [1986]. *The Medical Detectives, volume 2*, Washington Square Press.

Strunk, Jr., W. and E. B. White [1979]. *The Elements of Style*, Third Edition, Macmillan, New York, NY.

Tufte, E. R. [1983]. *The Visual Display of Quantitative Information*, Graphics Press, Cheshire, CN.

Strategic Imperatives in
Software Engineering Education

Harlan Mills
University of Florida and Information Systems Institute

Abstract

The strategic imperatives in software engineering education require that universities address the limits of human performance in the intellectual control of computer systems in industry and government. The remarkable growth in critical dependence of businesses and government agencies on computers in a single human generation presents unprecedented opportunities and challenges for educational institutions. Software development and maintenance seems a heuristic, error prone activity, much as doing arithmetic in roman numerals. Software engineering education must find the analogs of long division in place notation in software analysis and design. Such discoveries will change human capabilities as dramatically in software engineering as grade school students making calculations beyond Euclid's capability.

Defining Software Engineering as a University Subject

It seems clear that software engineering will become a widely accredited university subject. The intellectual content of university level work is emerging, beginning with fundamental work of Dijkstra, Parnas, Gries, Hoare, Wirth and others, and the need for university level work is evident in the size of the work force already involved with software in industry and government. The DoD support of the CMU SEI and its educational initiatives [Ford 87] reflects this judgement.

Exactly what software engineering will become as a university subject is yet to emerge over time. In the short run, people in the university and professional community will create the initial hypotheses to be tested, for example as found in [Ardis 85], [Gibbs 86], [Mills 80]. But the long run process that will determine the content of university level software engineering education in this country (in contrast with the process in the Soviet Union or Japan, for example) is quite different.

Universities will produce graduate software engineers for industry and government to hire, and the universities that produce the most marketable and effective such graduates will prosper in two ways. First, in the near term, student demands for entrance will be based on their prospective marketability as graduates, allowing continued curriculum and faculty development. Second, in the long term, alumni support by graduates who have been successful in industry and government will strengthen those programs that produced them. So the checks and balances of our free competitive society will determine the eventual definition of software engineering in university education.

While this process of the natural selection of an effective definition of a subject is common with many university subjects, such as accounting, mathematics, physics, medicine, electrical engineering, one additional aspect in software engineering seems unique. In most subjects, industry and government judge the quality and productivity of university graduates for the eventual prosperity of the universities that produce them from a position of economic and industrial independence. But in software engineering, because of the remarkable dependence of nearly all businesses of all industries on computer and information systems, the very survival and prosperity of these businesses will depend on the quality and productivity of the graduates they hire.

Software Engineering and Business Performance

The mobility of the Fortune 500 companies is well known. Even from decade to decade there is much movement among the places occupied in the 500. Some of this mobility is due to changing times. For example, airlines have replaced many railroads because of the changing transportation patterns. But most of this mobility is due to the managements of these companies. Good companies and managements adjust to changing times, and outdo competitors in present times. There was no law to prevent railroad companies from going into air transportation, but few did.

The widespread use and criticality of computer systems and software in business operations is accelerating this mobility and the rise and fall of individual companies. In the past, if top management wasn't too crisp or perceptive, middle management and corporate culture might still carry on in good style, because people are flexible in communications, in accepting and giving directives. But today, if top management picks the wrong computer systems, middle management can hardly undo the damage, because much of the corporate culture is now embedded in the wrong, inflexible computer systems that drive the day by day work. For example, fifteen years ago, a certain insurance company proudly declared in TV advertising that it was so people oriented it did not have any computers - clearly a top management decision. Those TV ads don't run any more, either because the company no longer exists or because it has changed its policy.

So businesses are not simply the judges of what effective software engineering practices will become. They are judged themselves every day in competition by the software engineering practices they use. This feedback process bodes well for the definition of software engineering that will emerge. It will not be the result of a popularity poll among economically independent companies. It will be determined by the companies that survive and prosper through the best use of software engineering in business competition.

Dealing with Business Change through Software

Forty years ago, any sizable, well managed business had strong systems and procedures groups, who translated management policies and strategies into orderly business processes for the day by day conduct of the business. This translation had the checks and balances of detailed observation and common sense of people who carried out the procedures defined. If, for example, such a procedure directed a clerk to make a paycheck for several million dollars to an hourly employee for the past weeks work, the clerk could be depended on to question such an operation. As a result, new management ideas could be readily translated into business action because of the fail safe nature of their implementations by people with common sense about what they were doing.

Today, such systems and procedures groups have been largely replaced by information systems analysts who translate management policies and strategies into computer software and users guides for more and more of the day by day conduct of the business. But in this translation, the computers offer no common sense such as people might. The million dollar paycheck is as easy to write as a hundred dollar paycheck, unless some computer programmer has thought to insert a condition to guard against such an event. While such a condition is possible, all the conditions that add up to the common sense of a human clerk are entirely beyond the state of art, even the most advanced artificial intelligence state of art, let alone a production business payroll system.

As a result of the lack of common sense of computers as agents of a business, the practice of management itself has changed dramatically. Whereas new ideas in business policies and strategies could be tried out in a fail safe way, incrementally and experimentally, in a natural selection process for improving business performance with systems and procedures groups in the past, such step by step adjustments are much less possible in a business highly dependent on computer systems. There are two reasons, based on the ease and safety of such adjustments.

First, it is easier to tell a clerk to try a new idea in business operations than to tell a computer. Usually a mere sketch of the idea in the business context will suffice, and with the common sense, even a misunderstanding would seldom be catastrophic. But to tell a computer to try a new idea requires a new or changed software definition that may involve hundreds or thousands of computer instructions and interact with thousands or millions of other instructions. So, instead of telling a clerk to try something new, system analysts and programmers need to do the translation through a change process of specification, design, implement, test, install that may take several people several weeks or months.

Second, it is safer to tell a clerk to try a new idea in business operations than to tell a computer. If the idea leads to unexpected anomalies, the clerk will notice, but the computer will not. Even with perfect software, a catastrophic event may take place if unusual conditions have not been entirely thought through. With software failures catastrophic events may take place unnoticed until too late to prevent or mitigate them. In either case, any prudent management gets very wary about changes in the computer systems without the fail safe operations possible with clerks and common sense.

Software as the Ultimate Bureaucracy

The consequence of these difficulties in dealing with change is that software has become the ultimate bureaucracy in business operations for two reasons. First, computers cannot adapt to people, so people must adapt to computers. While computers can be programmed to look more adaptable in one way or another, however they are programmed at the moment defines their exact behaviour to which people must adapt to use them. Second, as software gets more complex, it gets harder to change reliably. As a result, many line organizations, whose performance absolutely requires reliable computer operations and have seen computer outages from past well intentioned software change efforts, would rather live with old operative software than chance it with new software they can't count on. As traumatic as software change is to the developers, it is even more traumatic to the users for both these reasons.

In summary, the software bureaucracy resists change more than any people bureaucracy for good reason. And yet, business performance over time demands change to stay competitive. The value of good software engineering practices is to reduce the trauma of change, and it will show up in the very survival and prosperity of the businesses that employ them.

Human Data Processing and Automatic Data Processing

Computers are exciting already to many people. With the advent of small, inexpensive computers of remarkable power for local and personal use, a new generation is getting used to them very rapidly. The difficulty for businesses and governments is that these small personal computers helping individuals don't help very much at the total business or government levels. For example, an airline can't simply give a PC to each of its reservation clerks - that would surely create havoc in overbooked and underbooked flights. It might create a network of PCs for its clerks, but the state of art in distributed computing isn't up to that today, so it uses a central complex of mainframes to keep flight scheduling coherent, with all the problems of complexity that goes with it.

So the paradox is that people aren't really the problem in making use of computers - the businesses and governments have the problem of maintaining coherence over large domains of data processing. Businesses and governments have been operating hundreds of human generations, not just one as computers have. Before computers the term "data processing" had no specific meaning - people just ran departments, kept accounts, and did what data processing that was necessary in their heads, by pencil and paper, or most recently in history by hand calculators.

But with computers, data processing has come to mean something very specific. The processing of data is automatic, with no common sense or human checks between steps, and most of the data processing is for the benefit of automatic control rather than the human visible work. For example, it comes as a surprise to learn that one transaction (one data entry input to return one output response) by a reservation clerk requires many thousands of instructions to be executed by the computer complex. In order to check on the availability of seats in a specific flight, the clerk enters a few tens of characters, gets back a few tens of characters as the human visible content of the transaction. But each of the thousands of instructions may access more data than that, so most of the data processing is artificial to the human problem, but required for automatic processing - not twice or ten times as much, but literally thousands of times as much.

Now, consider the problem of managing the development and maintenance of the software that deals with the data of a business. Clearly, it is important to understand that data and how it is to be used in the business. But that isn't enough. Because for every instruction executed to deal with that business data, thousands of other instructions will be required to deal with the automatic processing of that business data. It is a mind expanding discovery that brings home the nature of the software problem. The data of the business are absolutely critical, but so is all the other data, used thousands of times as much as the business data.

So if one knows the business and its data needs well, but doesn't know the needs of automatic, no common sense, data processing, one has the recipe for endless frustration and competitive disaster. Yet, in an activity one generation old, there is little time tested precedent and procedure for predictable human performance as there is in business activities such as marketing or accounting.

Current Uses of Software Engineering

Faced with such demands for software development and maintenance,it might seem foregone that the very best of software engineering would be demanded and welcomed in business and government. But the facts seem to belie such common sense and logic. Even such a popularizer and persuader as Ed Yourdon seems puzzled that even the simplest, most easily explained structured methods have remarkably little use in the commercial software world [Yourdon86]. The study of Zelkowitz et al [Zelkowitz 84]indicated that even in the high tech end of the software industry, the methods were low tech in comparison with what is known professionally. Fred Brooks [Brooks 1987] begins the recent DSB report on Military Software with the statement,

"Many previous studies have provided an abundance of valid conclusions and detailed recommendations. Most remain unimplemented. If the military software problem is real, it is not perceived as urgent."

And the SDI Eastport report [SDI 1985] states,

"...the defense software industry is decades behind the state of art - an art only decades old."

It is all very surprising, until one remembers just how young software engineering is - at most a human generation. All this data processing is being done by necessity, not by voluntary choice by society. The pressures of business and military competition require it, but society is not prepared for it by tradition or precedent. When civil engineering was this age, the right triangle was yet to be discovered. But not much civil engineering had to be done. It took centuries after the invention of double entry accounting to see its general use.

As pointed out by Brooks, Yeh, Yourdon and others, there is a great deal more known about software engineering today than is used. The universities are capable of teaching much more technology, or could be with industry demands, than they do. The problem is more a management problem than a technology problem today. That doesn't make it easy, it makes it harder, because peoples lives and careers are at stake.

Moreover, computer and software systems are growing more complex in an ever accelerating way. In the beginning, each small system was isolated, running batches of input in regular sequences.More and more, systems are networks of mainframes, minis, micros,terminals both dumb and smart. And no simple sequences describe their operations. Furthermore, applications have piled up, often with scanty documentation to deal with changing times and conditions, so just keeping systems running can be a frustrating challenge that seems to require more luck than skill.

But while we have spent thirty years learning to manage this new technology, many of the critical principles and concepts needed for effective management have only emerged in the past five to fifteen years. So many people, particularly those in middle management, who learned the business fifteen or more years ago,have new things to learn to deal with the new complexities of the times. We know about old dogs and new tricks. But these old dogs also carry a good deal of experience and wisdom that younger ones haven't acquired. So it isn't useful just to move them out.Many can learn the new principles and concepts if given the chance. But one reason old dogs don't learn new tricks is that they don't believe they have the time, the opportunity to do so.

In summary, we have a new, immature industry growing so rapidly that it obsoletes people who don't grow themselves. Whereas a trade school knowledge was sufficient to deal with the early computer systems, it takes a university level knowledge for management and key technical people to work effectively with today's systems.

Measuring Human Performance in Software Engineering

The explosion of software development and maintenance in the past thirty years in the business world has no precedent in human history in the demands for people with new intellectual capabilities. The industrial revolution took centuries and called for one kind of work force with muscle. The information revolution is taking decades and calls for quite a different work force with brains. But as is becoming well apparent, it is harder to measure the performance of brain power than the performance of muscle power.

It has been well documented that there is a more than ten to one difference in productivity and quality of employed programmers in industry today. But it would seem such differences would be averaged out in large software groups in industry. After all,there are large differences in the heights and weights of people, but much smaller differences in the average heights and weights of large groups of people.

However, strange as it may seem, it has also been observed that this ten to one difference in productivity and quality exists in large software groups as well [Mills 1983] because of two reasons that do not hold for heights and weights. First, productivity and quality are not additive properties - one module plus one module can equal no system if they don't work together. Second, people do not join software groups at random, but through an offer/acceptance employment process. And the very managements who can make productivity and quality most additive through good software engineering practices, are those who can attract and employ the most productive and disciplined programmers. That is, good managements have it best both ways. This ten to one difference in large software groups has also been observed by DeMarco and Lister [DeMarco 1987].

The paradox with this difference in productivity and quality among software groups is that their general managements are frequently not able to recognize it in their own businesses. Each software group is doing unique work, which becomes part of the fabric of the business. All the common measures of productivity and quality can be easily gamed in front of general management. For example, lines of software code produced per person month is about as relevant to software productivity as words spoken per day to sales productivity. But there are better measures of sales productivity known to general management, so they don't use words spoken per day.

In fact, the poor performance groups are frequently regarded highly by their companies because they appear to be dedicated and working hard. For example, a group that comes in every weekend trying to get their system to run looks like it cares for the company - the reason may be poor work done earlier, but who knows that. And a group never in on weekends because its system runs with no problems may look like it should be working harder ("look at those people across the street!") - the reason is probably good work done earlier, but who knows that either.

While at first glance, this difficulty in assessing performance of software groups seems to lead to unfair results, there is a simple remedy for such aberrations. The companies with the best software groups are likely to survive and prosper against competitors with poor software groups, whether they recognize it or not. The presidents may get the credit, but the software groups will keep their jobs.

What Software Engineering Education Must Be

The foregoing trials and tribulations of an industrial society forced to conduct its business using computers and software for competitive reasons rather than tradition or precedent defines the challenge for software engineering education. Those companies that survive and prosper in industrial competition will eventually have a major say in what this education becomes. But they will survive and prosper in part on the basis of how well software engineering education has served them.

These trials and tribulations are due to the lack of intellectual and management control of computers and software today. The difference between ordinary human steps in conducting business and computer instruction steps is so great, and the number of computer steps required to simulate a human step is so large, that the usual methods of human thinking simply break down. Such an example of a change in step size occurred in arithmetic with the discovery of long division.

Before long division, numbers had to be treated as wholes, and good guessers were needed for division problems. But with long division, numbers could be treated at their component digit level. Well, roman numerals have digits, but long division is still impossible with roman numerals. It took the best and brightest of mankind thousands of years to discover the place notation that made long division possible. The use of a new digit zero for nothing was a critical discovery. So breaking division into the small steps of long division took a fundamental mathematical discovery to make it possible.

Had society tried to do as much arithmetic with roman numerals as software development and maintenance in the past 30 years, the consultants of the day would be involved in teaching people how to be better guessers in long division and square roots, and even just in adding long columns of numbers. But one can be sure that the conventional wisdom of these experts would be very similar to that of software today, namely that arithmetic is an error prone activity that takes could intuitive skills and is very difficult to manage to schedules and budgets. The great inventory after the Norman conquest was recorded in roman numerals, hamlet by hamlet,but never added up because of such wisdom.

With the benefit of a thousand years of hindsight, long division and square roots can be taught to children. It is a stepwise process with very small steps, multiplying and subtracting digit by digit with carries and borrows, putting the digits in the right places, but nothing bigger than digits. There is a small amount of guessing, to be sure, on what the next digit is to be. But the correctness of each guess is verified immediately in the next small step of the process, and can be corrected right then, if necessary. So long division is a formal stepwise refinement process with formal verification at each step. In such steps, there is little ego involved. If a mistake is made and pointed out, no feelings are hurt and the mistake readily corrected.

Before long division, no one realized that dividing whole numbers by whole numbers could be broken into smaller steps, nor that division was a large step. In hindsight we now realize it to be a large step.

Software engineering education must find the analog of long division in software analysis and design. Assembling instructions into programs was a large step, which Dijkstra and others showed how to break into small steps by the stepwise refinement of specifications into ultimate instructions. As in long division, each step can be verified immediately and corrected if necessary. But that seems to be a deep secret, even in most university software engineering curricula today. As pointed out in [Mills86] "While program correctness proofs are widely taught in universities for toy problems, most academics not deeply involved in the subject regard program correctness as academic." The idea of stepwise refinement is often discussed, but the deep idea of stepwise refinement with immediate verification is usually avoided. In long division the immediate verification is critical for getting correct answers, and so it is in program design, too.

Above the program level in modules (Ada packages, data abstractions, software objects), stepwise refinement is also critical, but discussed even less than for programs. Assembling modules or objects into systems are large steps, which can be broken into small steps by box structured analysis and design [Mills 1987]. Inventing the real time control of uses of a set of objects from a data flow diagram is a large step. Parnas showed how to develop usage hierarchies to break such problems into smaller steps [Parnas 79]. The immediate verification of each step is seldom discussed, but given in [Mills 87].

Software engineering today is often treated as an error prone human process. That will change as good methods are discovered and introduced. Division in roman numerals is an error prone process, but long division in place notation can be made as error free as desired with inspections and verifications, even though individuals are necessarily fallible. The evidence is that more than 90% of today's errors in software are due to faulty methods rather than faulty people [Mills 86]. Software engineering education will change human capabilities as dramatically as grade school students making calculations beyond Euclid's ability.

References

[Ardis 85]
Ardis, Mark, James Bouhana, Richard Fairley, Susan Gerhardt, Nancy Martin, and William McKeeman. Core Course Documentation: Master's Degree Program in Software Engineering. Tr-85-17, Wang Institute of Graduate Studies, September 1986

[Brooks 87]
Brooks, Frederick P. Jr. et al. Military Software. Defence Science Board, September 1987

[DeMarco 87]
DeMarco, Tom and Timothy Lister. Peopleware: Productive Projects and Teams. Doset House, 1987.

[Ford 87]
Ford, Gary, Norman Gibbs, James Tomayko. Software Engineering Education. CMU/SEI-87-TR-8, Software Engineering Institute, May 1987

[Gibbs 86]
Gibbs, Norman E., Richard E. Fairley, eds. Software Engineering Education: The Educational Needs of the Software Community. Springer-Verlag 1986

[Mills 80]
Mills, Harlan D. Software engineering education, Proc IEEE, V.68, n. 9, September 1980

[Mills 83]
Mills, Harlan D. Software Productivity, Little Brown 1983

[Mills 86]
Mills, Harlan D. Structured programming: retrospect and prospect. IEEE Software, November 1986

[Mills 87]
Mills, H. D., R. C. Linger, A. R. Hevner, Box structured information systems. IBM Systems Journal, V. 26, n. 4, 1987.

[Parnas 79]
Parnas, D. L. Designing software for ease of extension and contraction. IEEE Trans Software Engineering, SE-5 n. 3, March1979

[SDI 85]
Eastport Group, Report to the Director, SDIO, 1985

[Yourdon 86]
Yourdon, Edward N. Whatever happened to structured analysis? Datamation, V. 37, n. 1, June 1, 1987.

[Zelkowitz 84]
Zelkowitz, M. V., R. T. Yeh, R. G. Hamlet, J. D. Gannon, and V.R. Basili, Software engineering practices in the U. S. and Japan, Computer V. 17, n. 6, May 1984

Software Engineering in the Johns Hopkins University
Continuing Professional Programs

V.G. Sigillito (1,2), B.I. Blum (1) and P.H. Loy (2)

(1) Applied Physics Laboratory
(2) Whiting School of Engineering
The Johns Hopkins University

The need to educate computer professionals about the process, methods and tools used to create and maintain software systems is being met by The Johns Hopkins University at three levels. In the graduate program, which offers an M.S. in computer science to part-time students, a course in software engineering recently has been established as a degree requirement. At a second level, students in the program with an interest in software engineering may choose from a relatively comprehensive group of courses. Finally, at a third level, a short course program makes much of the same material available to non-matriculating professionals in a two to five full-day format. This paper describes the program, details the offerings, provides measures of the size and impact of the software engineering effort, and makes some general observations about the teaching of software engineering to practicing professionals.

BACKGROUND

Since its opening, The Johns Hopkins University has had the tradition of providing part-time education. Public lectures by faculty and visitors at Hopkins were a prominent feature of Baltimore's cultural life that predates radio. Formal courses and degree programs for part-time students, with courses held primarily in the evening, were established before World War I. It is in the context of this commitment to continuing education for practicing professionals that Johns Hopkins established what has become one of the nation's largest part-time graduate programs in computer science. In what follows, we outline the history of that program and show how it has been adapted to address professional needs in software engineering.

Origins of the Masters Degree Program

Starting with the 1964-65 academic year, the JHU Evening College (then known as the McCoy College) began offering courses leading to a masters of electrical engineering. These courses were held at the Applied Physics Laboratory, a division of the University located in a rural setting half-way between Baltimore and Washington. There were several reasons for selecting this site. First, the APL staff numbered over 2,000 people with an additional 1,000 on-site contractors. Thus, it was anticipated that APL would benefit directly from this program. Secondly, a large per capita proportion of the residents in the Baltimore-Washington corridor was made up of scientists and engineers. Consequently, a general need also was identified.

The emphasis of this masters program was the graduate training of practicing engineers. Very few of the graduates were expected to continue their education at the Ph.D. level. This emphasis on graduate education of practicing engineers and scientists remains a key feature of what has become five separate masters degree programs.

o   Electrical Engineering. This was the first of the part-time masters degree programs; it was begun in 1964-65.

o   Applied Mathematics. This was the first of the separate programs to be spun off; it was created in 1966-67.

o   Applied Physics. This program was established in 1967-68.

o   Computer Science. As will be discussed below, this program started in 1971-72.

o   Technical Management. This program was established in 1981-82.

In 1983, these programs were integrated into the Whiting School of Engineering as part of what now is called the Continuing Professional Programs.

The Computer Science Masters Degree Program

The first course in computer science, Numerical Analysis and Computer Science, was introduced in the 1966-67 academic year. This was a two semester course that covered topics in numerical analysis in the first semester and selected topics in programming techniques (mostly at the assembly language level) during the second semester. A course entitled Introduction to Computer Arts and Science, which concentrated on FORTRAN programming, was offered on the JHU Homewood campus in Baltimore.

These two were the only evening course offerings in computer science for the next four years. However, during that time there was a growing recognition of the need for advanced training in this new discipline. In particular, it was acknowledged that practicing engineers required special training to learn what was not taught at the time of their undergraduate education. Consequently, plans were made to institute a masters degree program in computer science. The program was introduced in the 1971-72 academic year. It offered the following mandatory (later called core) courses: operating systems, organization of data and files, programming languages, and computational models. The elective courses included numerical analysis, symbolic logic, probability and statistics as well as courses in operations research.

New computer science courses were introduced each year. The core courses, initially designed to provide a formal introduction to concepts that may not have been available when the student was an undergraduate, underwent continuing change as the students' undergraduate backgrounds improved. Course materials were upgraded, and some courses were replaced by an admission prerequisite or competency test. By 1979-80, there were 22 different computer science courses offered on a regular basis; many were available in multiple sections. Table 1 illustrates the growth of the program's offerings.

Course Category	79-80	80-81	81-82	82-83	83-84	84-85	85-86	86-87	87-88
Core Courses	3	4	4	4	4	4	4	4	4
Artificial Intel.	0	0	0	1	2	2	4	6	8
Computer Engineering	4	5	4	4	4	4	4	5	5
Computer Methodology	3	4	4	3	4	4	5	6	5
Computer Systems Org.	2	2	2	3	3	4	5	5	6
Info. and Database	2	3	3	3	3	3	3	3	3
Languages & Compilers	3	4	7	6	5	5	6	6	7
Software Engineering	2	2	1	2	4	5	7	7	8*
Theory of Computation	3	4	3	3	4	4	5	6	6
TOTAL	22	28	28	29	33	35	43	48	52

Table 1 Course Offerings in Computer Science by Year
* Does not include the software engineering core course.

Almost all the courses are given at the APL campus. This campus has 15 modern classrooms, each designed for thirty to thirty five students. (There are two sessions each evening, and each session meets once a week. Thus, this relatively small number of rooms is adequate for 150 class sections.) Although other rooms are available for larger groups, it is department policy to limit class size to thirty. The computing facilities at the APL campus consist of DEC VAX 11/780 and AT&T 3B20 processors, more than 100 terminals and workstations, and a large number of small computer systems. Microwave links provide access to the IBM 4341 and a variety of VAX 8600 and 11/750 systems located on the Homewood campus in Baltimore.

In 1986 a second campus dedicated to this program, the Montgomery County Center, was opened in a Maryland suburb of Washington. It currently is housed in temporary quarters, but a 20 class room facility is under construction. The new buildings will provide 38,000 square feet of usable space and will be situated in a 37 acre setting. There will be dedicated computational resources as well as access to the computers located at APL and Homewood. Table 2 indicates the size and impact of the program in terms of students, enrollment and degrees awarded. The table suggests that, despite the Montgomery County Center's temporary facilities, some students find it to be geographically more convenient; we expect the enrollment at that campus to increase significantly in the coming years.

The Johns Hopkins University also has two campuses in Baltimore that occasionally share the program's offerings. The Homewood campus is the location of the Schools of Engineering and Arts and Sciences; the medical institutions are situated in the East Baltimore campus. In 1984 a microwave link was installed so that the evening courses would be shared among all three campuses. Special classrooms are available on each campus that allow the two-way transmission of audio and video.

	78-79	79-80	80-81	81-82	82-83	83-84	84-85	85-86	86-87	87-88
Degree Candidates										
APL Campus	307	373	456	619	797	844	933	923	900	866
Montgomery Center									58	115
Class Enrollments										
APL Campus	1050	1366	1624	2246	2752	2924	2920	3040	2830	2854
Montgomery Center									432	582
Degrees Awarded	266*	84	104	117	128	214	237	240	262	---

Table 2 Evolution of the Computer Science Program
* Includes all Computer Science Masters Degrees prior to 1979

To meet the needs of professionals who are not part of a formal degree program, a short course program was instituted in 1985. The goal was to provide much of the same content that is available in degree programs in short, intensive, non-credit offerings. These courses are taught at the Parkway Center, which is located close to Baltimore-Washington International Airport and convenient to the hi-tech corridor along the Baltimore-Washington Parkway.

About half the students attending the short courses come from out of the area; some ten percent of the courses are presented on-site for an organization. The scope of the program's offerings in software engineering is shown in Table 3. There also are 13 other courses in artificial intelligence, engineering, communications, and performance evaluation. Eighty percent of the offerings are in computer science, and software engineering and artificial intelligence are the two fastest growing fields.

Course (Software Engineering Only)	85-86	86-87	87-88*
Software Testing and Quality Assurance	2	1	4
Structured Analysis and Design		1	1	1
Software Maintenance Techniques		1	1	1
Software Engineering: A Holistic Approach		1	1
Ada Software Development: A S.E. Approach		1	1
Engineering Software Quality		1	

Table 3 The Software Engineering Short Course Offerings by Year
* Includes announcements through March, 1988.

The Focus on Software Engineering

The first courses in software engineering were offered in the 1979-80 academic year. One of these courses, Structured Design, remains one of the most popular electives; it uses a case study to demonstrate the techniques of structured analysis and structured design. There have been a number of different instructors, and this year there are five sections. The second of those initial courses, Software Engineering for Real-Time Systems, was given only twice; in this case the instructor moved, and no adequate replacement could be found.

As shown in Table 4, the number of different courses grew starting in 1982-83. Program Development, Style, and Documentation was the first software engineering course to be offered at the 700 level. These courses are reserved for graduate degree candidates, and at least four of the ten courses required for graduation must be 700 level electives. The following year, two additional 700 level courses were introduced, and within another four years the program offered 22 sections of 9 different software engineering courses plus 17 sections of a new core course in software engineering. Table 5 displays the number of software engineering sections and students for 1987-88.

Course	Lev	Sections Offered								
		79-80	80-81	81-82	82-83	83-84	84-85	85-86	86-87	87-88
S.E. Real Time Sys	400	1	1							
Structured Design	400	1	2	2	2	2	3	2	4*	5*
Prog Lang, Style, Doc	700				1	1	1	1	1	1
Software Engineering	700					2	2	1	2*	3*
Software QA	700					1	1	1	1	1
S.E. with Ada	400							2	2	5*
Struct Testing & Main	400							1	3*	4
Modeling Real Time Sys	700							1	2	2
Fundamentals of S.E.	400									17*
Projects in S.E.	400									1
TOTALS		2	3	2	3	6	7	9	15*	39*

Table 4 Evolution of the Software Engineering Course Offerings
* Includes courses at the Montgomery County Center
400 level courses are for undergraduate and graduate students
700 level courses are for graduate students only

	Number of Sections	Number of Students
Foundations of S.E.	18	281
Projects in S.E.	1	9
Structured Design	6	124
S.E. with Ada	4	90
Struct Testing & Maintenance	4	88
Prog Lang, Style and Doc	1	30
Software Engineering	4	48
Software QA	1	12
Modeling Real Time Sys	2	82

Table 5 Software Engineering Enrollment, 1987-88 Academic Year

As the scope of the software engineering program broadened, it became clear to the Computer Science Program Committee (in the Continuing Professional Programs) that there was a need to expose all students to the fundamentals of software engineering. Consequently, it was decided that when the next core course was converted to an admission prerequisite a new software engineering requirement would take its place. Recall that the core courses were intended to provide a foundation for students (generally not computer science majors) who did not take those courses as undergraduates. Students with an undergraduate equivalent of a core course would not receive graduate credit for the core course should it be taken. Thus, the introduction of a new core requirement would guarantee that every graduate was familiar with the material it covered.

THE COURSE OFFERINGS

In this section we describe the three levels of software engineering offerings at The Johns Hopkins University. The next section makes some observations about the success of this program and discusses some issues that may be of interest to institutions that are facing similar demands.

Level 1. Foundations of Software Engineering

The first level of software engineering in the masters degree program is a core course called Foundations of Software Engineering. All newly enrolled students are expected to take this course unless, of course, they already have taken an equivalent course prior to admission. The course was designed by a two person team (not including any of the present authors) during the 1986-87 academic year. It was first offered in the fall of 1987. Clearly, it is premature for an evaluation of this course; we simply shall describe it.

The initial goal of the course designers was to bring together an overview of software engineering that could be taught from a text and supplemented with a class project and additional reading. A text, which was still in production, was chosen from a copy of its table of contents. Unfortunately, when the final text was delivered, it was seen immediately that it was too elementary for use in a graduate program. It then was decided to use Roger Pressman's, Software Engineering: A Practitioner's Approach, as the text. However, a syllabus was drawn up from the first edition just prior to the publication of the second (and considerably expanded) second edition. Consequently, the preparations for the new course were not as smooth as one would have hoped.

Because this new course was to be required of all new students, a large number of sections were planned. Unfortunately, many of the faculty advisers were not oriented properly, and many of the designated students did not sign up for the course. Course size ranged from 7 to 28. Several of the smaller sections were consolidated, but each of the 10 faculty members who prepared to teach the course had at least one section.

The catalog description and contents of the course are given in Figure 1. Obviously, there have been some start-up problems with this establishment of a software engineering prerequisite. A review of the instructors' experiences is scheduled for May, 1988, and we expect that our first year's experience will improve this offering in the years to come.

605.409 Foundations of Software Engineering

Fundamental software engineering techniques and methodologies required during the various phases of the software life cycle will be studied. Topics will include: requirements analysis, software design, programming methodology, testing, and maintenance. Emphasis will be placed on structured design techniques and programming methodology, including the use of top down design, logical models, data flow diagrams, pseudo-code, modularity, and other structured techniques. The importance of problem specification, programming style, documentation, maintainability, testing, and debugging techniques will be covered.

Prerequisite: 605.107 Introduction to Pascal Programming, or equivalent.

Text: "Software Engineering: A Practitioner's Approach", 2nd ed., Pressman, McGraw-Hill, 1987.

Course Outline

Introduction
The software lifecycle
Overview of software engineering
Goals
Principles
Tools

Requirements Analysis
Fundamentals
Requirements specification
Interface specification
Data flow methods
Data diagrams
Data dictionary
Data flow diagram tools
Data structure methods
Warnier-Orr diagrams
Jackson method
Concurrency issues
Quality assurrance issues

Software Design
Fundamentals
Modularity
Functional independence
Coupling
Cohesion
Overview of methodologies
Data flow oriented methods
Data structure oriented methods
Object oriented methods
Real-time methods and issues
Petri nets and data flow
Prototyping

System Development Example
Requirements to PDL

Coding
Structured coding methods
Coding conventions and style
Program "Builds"
Source code control
Libraries and separate compilation
Documentation

Testing Methodology
Test planning and data cases
Debugging
Test strategies
White box techniques
Black box techniques
Acceptance testing to requirements

Software Maintenance
Types of maintenance
State of the art of software maintenance
Design for maintenance
Tools for maintenance
Software management

Semester Project

Figure 1 Fundamentals of Software Engineering

Level 2. Software Engineering Electives

The organization of a balanced software engineering program in a part-time setting is particularly difficult. All faculty members have full-time employment outside the program, and -- given the limited salary -- few have the incentive to organize new courses beyond the area of their professional competence. Thus, while it may be possible to identify an appropriate course subject, it may not be possible always to find the qualified faculty. Conversely, there also is the continuing need to adjust the program as a field changes. Frequently, this involves terminating or redirecting a course or turning down an offer to teach a course that does not fit in with the rest of the program.

Recognizing the limitations in designing a balanced program in this setting, we nevertheless feel that we have a comprehensive set of offerings for a masters degree program. Although this is subject to change based upon our review of the Fundamentals of Software Engineering experience, our current electives are as follows.

Structured Design. This is a 400 level introductory course based upon the work of Constantine, Myers, Yourdon, etc. Various texts have been used.

Software Engineering with Ada. This is a 400 level course that serves to introduce the Ada programming language and how it is used to support the software process. As the title suggests, Booch is the text.

Structured Testing and Maintenance. This is a 400 level course designed to present an overview of verification and validation. Beizer's Software Testing Techniques generally is used as the text.

Projects in Software Engineering. This 400 level course is designed around a class project. Students will be expected to select from existing standards and demonstrate an understanding of the methods and tools used in large project development. It will be offered in the Spring 1988 term for the first time.

Program Development, Style, and Documentation. This is the first of the 700 level courses. It was designed to show how the use of UNIX tools could support an integrated environment that facilitated good software engineering practices. This course may be integrated with the new "topics" course.

Software Quality Assurance. This 700 level course has Structured Testing and Maintenance as a prerequisite. It covers a review of techniques, software integration, reliability models, and QA plans.

Modeling Real-Time Systems. This 700 level course has Structured Design as a prerequisite. It addresses methods and tools to manage performance constraints, partitioning, hardware allocation, and design and implementation tradeoffs.

Software Engineering. This 700 level course will be renamed Advanced Topics in Software Engineering. The course provides an overview of software engineering with an emphasis on research topics. The major student activity is the preparation of a term paper. Typical class size is 25-30 students; thus, a true seminar is not practical.

Level 3. Short Courses

The short course offerings in software engineering reflect our assessment of industry's demand for certain courses as limited by our ability to find qualified instructors for them. Unlike the masters degree program, however, the short course program is not constrained by a need to maintain a balanced or comprehensive program; its students are not pursuing a course of study leading to a degree. Nevertheless, we do strive to provide as wide a range of offerings as our resources permit.

We currently offer the following software engineering courses. Most courses cover material taught in a graduate degree course, and most of the short course faculty teach a similar course in the masters degree program.

Software Testing and Quality Assurance. This two-day course stresses the importance of developing a comprehensive testing strategy, the roles that QA and testing play in the development life cycle, and the relationships between QA functions and testing activities. It also provides heuristic approaches for test planning and creating test cases. Beizer is used as the text.

Structured Analysis and Design. This is a five-day course that is very similar in content to the graduate course Structured Design. It now includes hands-on experience with a CASE tool. DeMarco is used as the text.

Software Maintenance Techniques. This three-day course covers the problems and pitfalls of maintenance, and the techniques that address those problems, from both a technical and managerial point-of-view. The Martin and McClure book on software maintenance is used as the text.

Software Engineering: A Holistic Approach. This three-day course is the most comprehensive software engineering offering in the short course curriculum. It presents an overview of software development and maintenance from both a technical and historic perspective, and it summarizes some of the most promising areas of current research. Fairley is used as the text.

Ada Software Development: A Software Engineering Approach. This three-day course is aimed at helping designers and programmers exploit the features of the Ada language to the fullest by using the concepts of object-oriented design. Booch is used as the text.

Engineering Software Quality: A Preemptive Strategy. This is a new three-day course that stresses the relationships among the different facets of development and the quality of the final product. Technical, managerial, business, social, political, and engineering issues are dealt with in the context of the software development environment.

DISCUSSION

The computer science masters degree program at The Johns Hopkins University is one of the largest such programs in the nation. We have shown how it has evolved over time to meet the changing needs of the local professional community. Like many educational programs, it offers a growing diversity of courses. However, two topics have elicited a great deal of student (and industry) interest and have lead to an extraordinary response. These are software engineering and artificial intelligence. As Table 1 illustrates, the program has been able to accommodate this demand.

We believe that one of the contributions of this paper is the demonstration that it is possible for a computer science department to meet the changing educational needs of its students rapidly and effectively. We further believe that our experience with these courses (as shown in Tables 4 and 5) provides a clear proof that there is an interest in and perceived need for a program in software engineering.

We also observe that there are distinct differences between part-time and full-time faculties. Although a few full-time faculty members participate in the part-time program, most of the faculty must be recruited from outside the full-time departments. Fortunately, we have been able to build up an effective software engineering faculty. As shown in Table 6, about half of the instructors work for some division of the Johns Hopkins University, the other half work in industry. Very few of the faculty members are engaged in research in computer science, but most apply their postgraduate training in their work.

Faculty Education and Employment	Advanced S.E. Courses	Core S.E. Course
Doctoral degrees	7	3
Masters degrees *		
JHU	3	5
Other	4	3
Employment		
APL	5	3
Other JHU Divisions	1	1
Industry	6	6
Government	1	1
Total S.E. faculty **	13	11

Table 6 Software Engineering Faculty Characteristics

* Includes masters degrees granted after another graduate degree.
** Some members are counted in both columns.

For a program oriented to practitioners, there are many advantages to having a part-time faculty. These instructors can offer both an academic and professional perspective; their areas of interest generally overlap with those of the student population; and their low (relative to their full time employment) salaries and insignificant titles imply a commitment to the joy of teaching. On the other hand, as a program becomes more specialized, finding the appropriate faculty becomes more difficult.

With respect to the program's software engineering offerings, we believe that there also are differences between a part-time and full-time (graduate or undergraduate) program. In a full-time program, the assumption is that the students have spent most of their academic careers working independently. Therefore, one of the goals of a software engineering course is to engage the students in a cooperative activity by means of a class project. In a part-time graduate program, on the other hand, it can be assumed that most of the students are professional programmers, analysts, software engineers, etc. In this case, the class projects of the 400 level courses are used to build upon the students' experience; the instructors emphasize the application of the methods and tools while drawing upon the students' at-work experiences.

Because we assume that most students have "real world" experience, our part-time courses are structured differently. The two general software engineering courses (the 400 level Fundamentals and the 700 level Software Engineering) offer contrasting approaches to meeting the students' needs.

The 700 level course was designed by one of the authors (BIB) to expose the students to a seminar-like experience. (Unlike students in a Ph.D. program, part-time students have few opportunities to learn how to perform research.) For this advanced course, structured design was a prerequisite, and it was assumed that the students were familiar with the fundamentals of software engineering. Therefore, the sessions focused on the discussion of software engineering topics at a level appropriate for masters degree students. A text was used, but no attempt was made to coordinate the students' reading assignments with the topics discussed in class. The main activity was independent reading, participation in class lectures and discussion, and the preparation of a term paper. There was no class project, and the term paper grade was the major determinant of the final grade.

The advanced software engineering course just described was intended to build upon the backgrounds of the students. In that sense, it was a "context" course designed to afford a context for the facts and knowledge that the students were assumed to have already. However, when the same author taught the fundamentals (or 400 level core) course, it was taught as a "content" course. Here the goal was to expose the students to software engineering with the assumption that this would be the students' first systematic exposure to the discipline. Each student was expected to leave the course with a basic set of skills (such as being able to draw accurate data flow diagrams) and a knowledge of some broadly accepted concepts and definitions. A class project was used to reinforce the material taught.

Thus, even though the two courses may have had similar content, they were quite different in structure and intent. The objective of the core, or "content" course was to establish a foundation for the students' subsequent graduate software engineering education. The objective of the advanced, or "context" course, on the other hand, was to tie together the various threads of the students' graduate education and offer some insight into the directions of software engineering research. Ideally, the students will use the skills learned in the core course throughout their education and work experience; they may not recognize the value of the second course until years after they have been granted their degrees.

Having described our program and the variety of our offerings, we feel that we also should discuss our views on a masters degree program in software engineering. We have shown in our historical introduction that JHU has precedent for spinning off independent programs; five such masters degree programs currently exist. It is the consensus of the Computer Science Program Committee, however, that this should not be done for software engineering. To us, software engineering is a subdiscipline of computer science. Most areas of software engineering research -- particularly with respect to formal methods-- belong to computer science. Thus, it is our perception that the separation of software engineering from computer science would tend to destroy its intellectual foundations. The division also would remove a very important part of the computer science curriculum.

That is not to suggest that a software engineering program, such as the one that existed at the Wang Institute, could not be a viable program; it will teach computer science from a software engineering perspective. But that is not the path we have chosen. For us, the extraction of software engineering from a computer science program would remove the symbiotic effects that we believe contribute to the success of our program. We encourage our students to begin with a focused group of courses and then add some electives outside that focus. Consequently, even though we are establishing a software engineering track, we expect the students to take other computer science courses as well.

Like most effective educational programs, ours is in a state of change. There is much for us to learn from our first year of experience with the Fundamentals of Software Engineering course. We also plan to review our other offerings in software engineering to reassure ourselves that we have a balanced program without too many overlaps or omissions. Finally, we are experimenting with the use of course material developed for the SEI Video Dissemination Project, and we will be offering the Formal Methods course this spring as a non-credit adjunct to our program.

We will be revising our software engineering syllabi in the next term, and we will be happy to make them available to other institutions with similar needs or interests.

Meeting the Training Needs of Practicing Software Engineers at Texas Instruments

Freeman L. Moore

Phillip R. Purvis

Texas Instruments Incorporated

Dallas, Texas

Abstract. *Much has been written about software engineering programs from the viewpoint of the academician, but do these programs really reflect the needs of industry? This paper provides some insight into the needs of practicing software engineers at Texas Instruments who are developing software according to military specifications and requirements for embedded real-time systems. The needs of our environment are compared to the entering skills of a typical new-hire, with the differences noted. These differences can be satisfied by internal training that covers all aspects of software engineering, from communicating with co-workers to understanding the system life cycle.*

1. INTRODUCTION

What does a practicing software engineer really need? That question and its answers have formed the basis for numerous discussions by a variety of individuals in several forums [1]. While this question has been debated heavily in the academic community, the real audience is the industrial environment that ultimately hires graduates from college programs. Thus, the key part of the question is on *practicing* from the perspective of an employer. In this case, the employer is a developer of software for defense systems.

Texas Instruments is a large company with several in-house training departments addressing the various needs of the company. Texas Instruments as a company is concerned with the quality of the product that it develops, and recognizes that the product is a reflection of the abilities of the individuals working on it. There has been a recent movement within the company to recognize the importance of organized training efforts with a goal of supporting software engineering. This paper will discuss some of the topics identified as necessary for the software engineer to maintain expertise within the domain of developing software for a defense contractor.

Texas Instruments is composed of several major groups. This paper is written from the perspective of the Defense Systems and Electronics Group (DSEG). As such, software development concerns will focus on the application of military standards (MIL-STD) during the software development process. The authors are members of the Computer Systems Training organization, a branch of the Human Resources Development Department. This department is supported by a staff of professionals who develop, maintain, and deliver a varied curriculum to the Texas Instruments scientific community (primarily DSEG). This training organization is described in detail in Section 5.

2. WHAT IS REALLY NEEDED?

Most of the software development in DSEG supports embedded microprocessor systems running in a real-time environment. As a general rule, the MIL-STD-1750A processor is used although other microprocessors are being introduced. The MIL-STD-1750A is a 16-bit instruction set architecture, developed by the Air Force. Within DSEG, there are many diverse projects, working under an everchanging set of requirements, developed according to military standard specifications and documentation requirements. The primary deliverables are systems composed of both hardware and software. Often, software engineers have no exposure to the intended hardware environment until system integration and testing.

In addition to software development for real-time systems, internal support software is used heavily. In some cases, specialized software for hardware simulation, distributed operating systems, and even compilers are developed by software engineers to meet the unique requirements of a given project.

The job of a "software design engineer" entails much more than simply writing software. The software engineer must function in a development team environment. Team members typically include software technicians, lead engineers, members of software quality assurance (SQA), software configuration management (SCM), software management, and project management. The software engineer must also interact with the customer. Communication skills are essential during requirements analysis and design reviews when the software engineer must identify and interpret customer requirements. Both environments require effective communication skills and the ability to work as a team. Briefly stated, a DSEG software engineer needs:

- an understanding of software development techniques,
- technical skills in software design,
- an understanding of hardware/software testing methodologies,
- technical skills in software implementation and testing,
- an understanding of real-time hardware/software interaction,

- an understanding of MIL-STD requirements, and

- communication skills (oral/written).

Ideally, DSEG would prefer that new employees were productive from the very first day of employment. However, we find that in many cases, college graduates are not familiar with the challenges of developing software in a defense contractor environment. Employers often hire individuals because of the perceived potential to adapt to new environments and to bring new ideas to the workplace. We have found that assistance must be provided in understanding the Texas Instruments work environment, and in particular, DSEG project needs.

Once we have identified the skills that are required of a software engineer, we have to determine what knowledge and skills exist in a software professional hired into DSEG. With this information, appropriate training can be identified to assist in the transition from college graduate to practicing software engineer.

3. WHAT DO SOFTWARE GRADUATES HAVE UPON ENTRY TO DSEG?

In DSEG, the **Software Engineering Workshop** provides a vehicle for viewing the background and capabilities of newly hired software engineers. This course, detailed in section 5, has been conducted with over 250 students during the past two years. Observations from instructors as well as comments from students have generated the following informal statistics about attendees:

- Generally, students lack the ability to apply a design methodology to an assigned problem (especially using graphics other than a flowchart).

- About 25% of the people have not had a course in software engineering (this includes several persons recently out of the armed forces who graduated 4-6 years ago).

- Very few have had any embedded real-time course work.

- Very few have heard of SQA and SCM. Of those who have, a minimal number remember the role of SQA and SCM in the development process.

- Most professional hires have had good experience in software engineering, but lack the terminology to map their concepts and experiences to a DoD development environment.

- Software testing experiences vary tremendously.

- Over 50% have had technical writing courses.

- About 20% have had public speaking courses/experiences.

- Most graduates with a degree in Electrical or Computer Engineering have not had any software engineering courses focusing on requirements analysis and design.

According to a recent survey of courses in software engineering education [2], 80% of the larger institutions offer software engineering courses while only half of the smaller schools have this type of course(s). Three quarters of the courses are general in nature, with at least one half of them offered at the undergraduate level. This survey was distributed to 200 universities considered likely candidates to offer software engineering classes. Ninety-five universities (48%) responded to the survey. Similar results are reported in the Leventhal article [3].

With our observations as well as those noted in Werth's article [2], we can draw some conclusions:

- Most graduates have a general understanding of the software development life cycle.

- Most graduates do not have a good understanding of the details of each "phase" of the software development process, except for coding.

- More graduates are learning how to write better technical documentation before they enter industry.

- Few graduates have experience in formatting information for presentations or in conducting a presentation.

- The terminology and toolsets that a person brings to DSEG seem as varied as the number of IBM compatibles currently on the market.

Now that we have discussed the skills needed by a practicing software engineer and the beginning skills and knowledge of a recently hired software professional, the differences can be noted. These differences serve as a basis for training and education opportunities to maintain and improve the quality of practicing software engineers. The next section suggests how universities can help students improve the transition from academe to industry. Section 5 describes how DSEG is currently improving the quality of its practicing software engineers.

4. HOW CAN UNIVERSITIES HELP TO IMPROVE THE QUALITY OF GRADUATES?

The unfulfilled needs of practicing DSEG software engineers can be determined by finding the differences between needs and entering skills as noted in sections 2 and 3 above. These differences are identified, and recommendations are made to the universities as the source of this education and training.

A major difference occurs in the area of practical experience. This type of knowledge and skill can be obtained best from on-the-job activities. While a majority of this education and training must occur after the person has been employed, universities should encourage students to participate in course projects and co-operative internship programs. These programs provide good experience during the college years.

Knowledge and skills with software toolsets is another difference encountered. Software toolsets include computer systems and software development tools (e.g., editors, compilers, linkers, debuggers, etc.). Industry must continue to train its employees in company specifics. Industry can reduce or eliminate training in those areas that are adequately taught in university courses. For example, Pascal was the primary language taught in DSEG four years ago. The course is no longer offered on a regular basis because of the training that students receive in college.

Technical writing is required of all DSEG software engineers at some time during their career. Some colleges offer technical writing courses. It is our recommendation that colleges *require* these courses of students entering into the software profession.

Making formal presentations is another requirement that DSEG software engineers will encounter in their career. Practical experience is a key to learning these skills. However, courses geared to taking information from a document and presenting it in an understandable and concise format is feasible at the university level. This ability, combined with public speaking skills, is a major benefit to the software engineer.

Another major difference is in the area of development, that is, analysis, design, and testing methodologies. Again, industry must train the employees in the specifics, but universities can present general overviews of most of the methodologies. Detail of at least one of the methodologies must be given in order for the students to obtain the most beneficial knowledge. It is critical for a software engineer in DSEG to choose an effective development methodology depending on current requirements. The requirements will vary for the engineer who has the opportunity to work on projects in each phase of the system life cycle (i.e., concept exploration, demonstration and validation, full scale development, and production and deployment).

Real-time systems development is a major activity in DSEG and in other companies. Courses in real-time design and programming may not be available at some colleges and universities. The specifics (e.g., target processors, application technologies, etc.) must be taught at the hiring company, but common topics can be identified and offered as an elective to the student on campus.

New software engineers have little experience in working effectively with other people on a software project. The roles of various people in a software development effort varies from company to company and are learned once the person comes on board. Excellent progress has been made in reducing this gap at the university level. Jim Tomayko presented a course model [4] at a recent conference on software engineering education. This model represents an excellent example of allowing the students to experience roles related to software quality assurance, software configuration management, software development personnel, project management, and the customer.

5. HOW DOES DSEG IMPROVE THE QUALITY OF PRACTICING SOFTWARE ENGINEERS?

This section is divided into four sub-sections to describe the training and education opportunities available to a practicing software engineer employed by DSEG. The sub-sections list the characteristics of DSEG that affect training, the DSEG training organization, a summary of the DSEG software curriculum, and a scenario of a software engineer utilizing the DSEG training opportunities.

5.1 THE CHARACTERISTICS OF DSEG THAT AFFECT TRAINING

DSEG is one of the largest groups that comprise Texas Instruments. DSEG is organized into several business entities that address specific needs, such as electro-optics, avionics, and missile systems. Upon joining the company, an individual is expected to be productive in a short amount of time. On-the-job-training (OJT) has historically been considered as the primary means of learning one's job. On-the-job-training is beneficial, in that, it keeps the individual within the work area and not away in a classroom. This allows the individual to combine learning with working. Unfortunately, OJT often times is not a very good means of learning information.It can be hit-and-miss, not well organized, or incomplete. In the long run, the individual depending upon OJT could take longer to learn the material than if a course had been attended.

Texas Instruments may have major contracts totalling in the millions of dollars, and at the same time relatively small contracts. Large contracts may explicitly include training as a budgetary item, whereas small contracts may not allow for training. Time is another variable that comes into play. Some managers believe that time cannot be spared for training, especially if tight schedules are imposed. Thus, there may be a reluctance to formal training, resulting in greater use of OJT (and minimal time away from the job).

Another concern about training is the turnover of people in the training audience. An engineer may be associated with a given project for 12 to 24 months and then move onto a different project with different requirements. This type of internal movement is encouraged, but at the same time, introduces the additional burden of identifying the timeliness of training that may be needed for engineers on a project. While some aspects of software development have been standardized, there is still a great deal of flexibility between the various business entities.

5.2 THE DSEG TRAINING ORGANIZATION

DSEG's primary training organization is known as the Human Resources Development Department (HRD). This department is tasked to provide training to persons in all major job families (e.g., mechanical, electrical, software engineering, etc.). The four major branches of this department are Computer Systems Training, Engineering Training, Management Development, and Group Education Administration.

Computer Systems Training exists to improve human performance in the efficient use of existing computer tools and new technologies which support DSEG requirements. The key thrust areas are Ada, software engineering, microprocessors, and artificial intelligence.

The Engineering Training Branch provides curriculum development, delivery, and administration in response to the defined needs of the business entities. Course emphasis is placed upon those topics common to current DSEG engineering disciplines: Computer Aided Design, Electrical Engineering, and Mechanical Engineering.

The mission of the Management Development Branch is to help DSEG supervisors and managers acquire the knowledge, skills, attitudes, and tools to successfully attain business objectives by effectively managing the work of others. Leadership development courses help managers perform their jobs better, and specific skills training can be taken for specialized needs.

Group Education Administration is responsible for education programs that are primarily external to the group. This includes Site Training & Education and the administration of Development Programs (defined below).

Each Site Training and Education administrator is responsible for providing the following information to employees:

- Educational Assistance - This program is designed to aid the employee in obtaining continuing professional and technical education through university and college programs.

- Association for Higher Education (TAGER) - On-site extension of the Educational Assistance program to provide live classroom instruction via video and talkback to major area universities.

- Professional Seminars (Out of Plant training) - Provide for professional growth through seminars and workshops not available through Educational Assistance.

- Professional Society Memberships - This program encourages professional employees to maintain contact with their profession through a society membership.

The Development Programs include:

- CO-OP - A program that offers full-time employment alternating with full-time academic terms at universities with cooperative education programs.

- SEP - The Summer Engineering Program offers full-time employment to outstanding students following their junior year in college.

- ESDP - The Engineering and Science Development Program offers half-time work and half-time school to qualifying and accepted employees.

In August of 1987, DSEG adopted a standard procedure to ensure that managers in the various business entities provide all employees with training and education that will enable them to meet both current and anticipated job requirements. This standard procedure represents a giant step toward providing individuals with more appropriate and timely training. Training models have been developed for major job classes by each business entity. A job class corresponds to the job title (e.g., software design engineer, software systems engineer) within a job family (e.g., software engineer). Plans are in place to include the remaining DSEG population in subsequent models. This model specifies a set of required courses and optional courses to be taken within the first three years of employment in DSEG.

There are also other training organizations available in Texas Instruments for the DSEG employee. Most widely used among the software engineering personnel are the Corporate Technical Education courses. These courses are usually one to two months in length with instructors from area universities or consulting firms.

5.3 A SUMMARY OF THE DSEG SOFTWARE CURRICULUM.

Figure 1 represents the basic training model for software engineers. This training model includes courses that are currently being offered by the Computer Systems Training branch of HRD and support software engineering goals as defined by our Computer Aided Software Engineering (CASE) steering committee. This training model was provided as input to each business entity in preparation of specific training models developed by the entity. A description of the major courses available from Computer Systems Training is provided below.

The Software Engineering Workshop is a three-day course to assist software, electrical, and mechanical engineers who are developing software. The course introduces DSEG software practices, standards, and DoD-STD-2167 [5] life cycle requirements. Participants work in teams to analyze actual project documentation, write portions of a requirement specification, and participate in a Software Specification Review.

An SQA Orientation Class is available for software quality assurance engineers after attending the Software Engineering Workshop. This is a three-day course which intro-

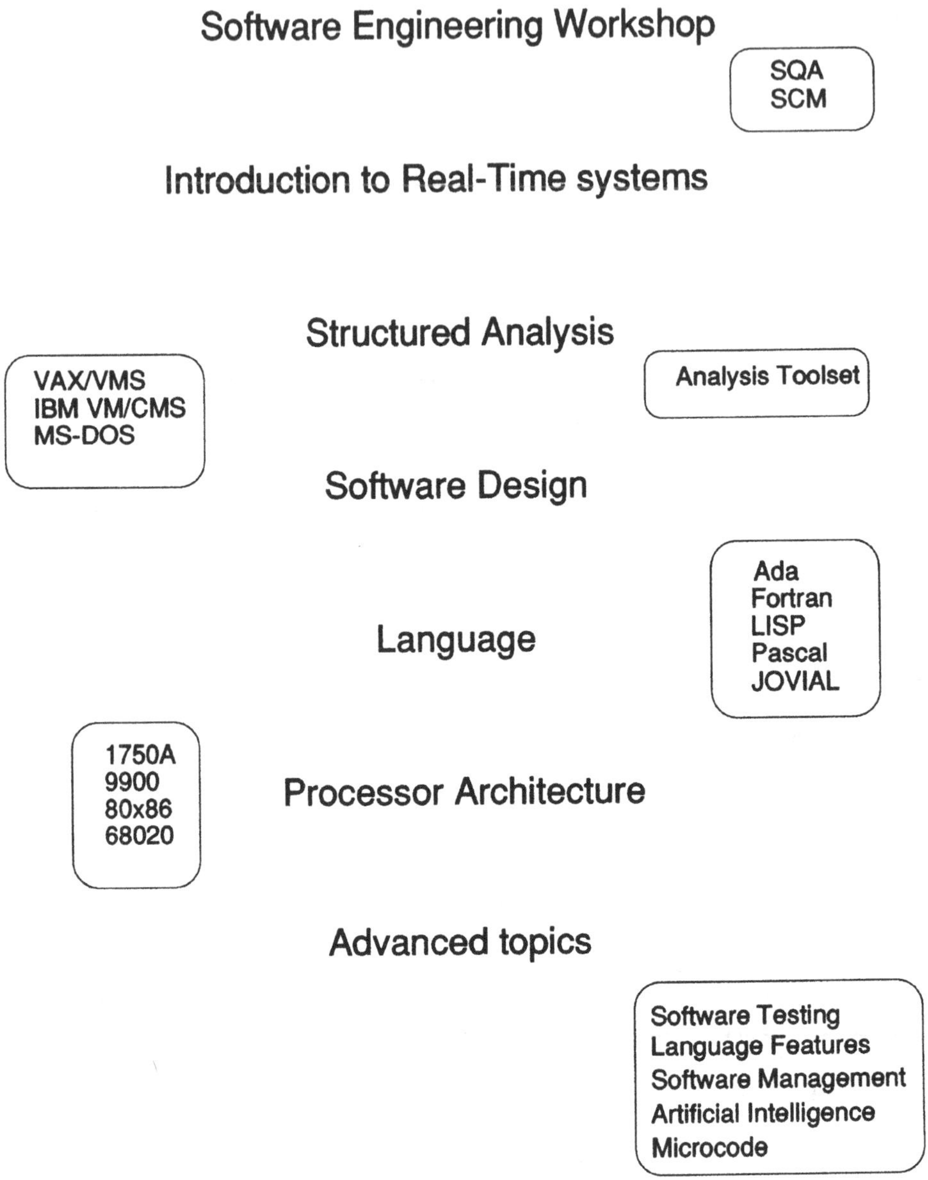

Software Engineering Workshop

SQA
SCM

Introduction to Real-Time systems

Structured Analysis

VAX/VMS
IBM VM/CMS
MS-DOS

Analysis Toolset

Software Design

Language

Ada
Fortran
LISP
Pascal
JOVIAL

1750A
9900
80x86
68020

Processor Architecture

Advanced topics

Software Testing
Language Features
Software Management
Artificial Intelligence
Microcode

Figure 1 - Basic Training Model

duces the attendee to SQA practices in the product life cycle. Participants work in teams to define evaluation criteria, audit test results, trace test requirements to requirements specifications, and evaluate an approved SQA plan.

An SCM Orientation Class is funded for development in 1988. This course(s) will provide software configuration managers and technicians with the knowledge and skills to more effectively identify, control, account for, and review configuration items.

There are several computer system classes that introduce the participant to the operating systems used in DSEG. Most of these systems have an introductory course and an advanced course. These courses provide information on how to log on and off; create, modify, and copy files; compile, link, and execute programs; and use operating system utilities and command languages to tailor individual computer accounts to specific project needs. Course deliveries average two days.

Real-time principles are fundamental to software development performed within DSEG. Computer Systems Training provides a "Introduction to Real-Time Systems" course to supply the necessary background to those engineers who need it. Other courses deal with the architecture issues of a MIL-STD-1750A processor, as well as how to microprogram array processors that are used by some projects.

As part of standardizing software development, the DSEG CASE steering committee has recognized the importance of establishing a sound beginning, starting with real-time structured analysis. Our approach is based upon work done by Paul Ward and documented in his books [6]. The Real-Time Structured Analysis course was recently introduced and has received a great deal of interest. We will be following this course with a structured design course tailored for our environment.

CASE toolsets are gaining acceptance, and credibility in the software design community. Software engineers are now using software that costs more than the hardware it runs on. CASE toolsets help automate some of the work involved in documenting the products of structured analysis and design. The toolsets can even provide some help in code generation and producing military standard documentation. A hands-on course is available that introduces the capabilities of a CASE toolset to a software engineer.

Since 1983, the Ada curriculum has been in existence to provide training in the language, stressing proper software development (not simply syntax). Advanced courses have been introduced with the current development effort being a course which presents the implementation characteristics of a compiler with respect to a given hardware architecture. Because of recent Department of Defense directives, greater interest in using Ada by various projects within DSEG is expected.

The Software Engineering Project Management course helps software managers and lead engineers to plan, budget, and control software projects. The course utilizes case studies and handouts that deal with typical software life-cycle deliverables in conformance with DSEG software methodology and the DoD acquisition cycle.

Artificial Intelligence (AI) training is currently limited to symbolic programming languages, expert systems, and the Explorer™ Lisp Machine. Texas Instruments has been researching artificial intelligence for many years, and DSEG established an AI lab to develop applications for use by the DoD. These courses were developed to meet specific DSEG requirements identified by the AI Lab. Several AI courses are offered by other training groups within Texas Instruments.

5.4 A SCENARIO.

Consider how a typical software engineer might be affected by DSEG training opportunities:

Kim Jones graduated with a Bachelor's degree in computer science in 1985. This degree required two co-operative internships (each being one semester in length). Kim was employed by the Automated Engineering Technology division of Southwestern Enterprises for the duration of both internships. Kim's primary responsibility was working with engineers to obtain requirements for special purpose software applications. These applications were implemented using the C language on a TOKUNGFU Personal Computer.

During Kim's campus interviews, the DSEG software recruiter (a practicing software engineer), was impressed with Kim's experience during the co-ops. Kim had performed well in college and answered all the recruiter's questions with multiple sentences. Kim's resume was very well organized and concise. The software recruiter gave Kim a very good evaluation. Subsequently, a hiring supervisor from the Missile Systems business entity invited Kim in for a plant visit. Kim was a perfect match for the job and accepted the offer.

After being on the job for a month, a fellow practicing software engineer invited Kim to a CDR to review the SDDD, STDs, and updates to the STLDD, SRS, and SDP. Kim was told that an SQA engineer would be there and to get the most recent version of the SDDD from SCM. Did Kim go into massive panic mode? NO! Having attended the Software Engineering Workshop (SEW) two weeks earlier, Kim was able to remember some of the acronyms. Kim referenced the SEW notebook for an explanation of other acronyms. Kim then knew the meaning of the acronyms, understood how everything interrelated, and what to expect at the CDR.

Kim was pleased to find that DSEG would reimburse her membership to a professional society. Kim was very interested in keeping up to date on the latest techniques in software engineering. The professional society also conducted a seminar on software metrics that Kim was allowed to attend. This seminar provided useful information for Kim's project to gather useful development statistics.

During the rest of the year, Kim attended several more classes. One class provided the knowledge and experience to utilize the VAX/VMS™ operating system. Kim attended an Ada class when the project received a new government contract. The Ada class presented software engineering design issues and a design methodology known as object-oriented design.

After being employed in DSEG for a year, Kim wanted to pursue an advanced degree. Kim's supervisor and site training personnel agreed that this was in the best interest of all involved, and encouraged Kim to enroll at a local university. During the course of earning a Master's degree in computer science, Kim took some classes at Texas Instruments over the TAGER network.

For the next few years, Kim will continue to take courses in real-time, structured analysis and design, effective communications & presentations, and software project management. The DSEG courses will be supplemented by external training as necessary. These training and education opportunities as well as Kim's desire to *be the best you can be* will guarantee a quality practicing software engineer for Texas Instruments.

6. CONCLUSIONS

This scenario illustrates the assistance that is available to employees to help them fully understand their jobs. We have attempted to show that new employees are provided with training to supplement their college background in topics specific to the DSEG domain, namely embedded real-time software development according to military specifications and requirements.

We have provided education and training recommendations to universities. We believe these recommendations are applicable to most industries performing software development. In the relationship of industry as a customer of the university, our desire is that the universities and industry communicate effectively in the on-going validation of customer needs.

We fully support the efforts of various college programs and their introduction of software engineering in the computer science and computer engineering curriculums. We realize that no program can be complete, and that it is the job of industry to "fine-tune" that training for the specific needs of the job that a person is performing.

7. REFERENCES

[1] P. Freeman, "Essential Elements of Software Engineering Revisited," *IEEE Transactions on Software Engineering*, vol. 13, no. 11, November 1987.

[2] L. Werth, "Software Engineering Education: A Survey of Current Courses," *ACM Software Engineering Notes*, vol. 12, no. 4, October 1987.

[3] L. Leventhal and B. Mynatt, "Components of Typical Undergraduate Software Engineering Courses: Results from a Survey," *IEEE Transactions on Software Engineering*, vol 13, no. 11, November 1987.

[4] J. Tomayko, "Teaching a Project-Intensive Introduction to Software Engineering," SEI-87-SR-1, Software Engineering Institute, Carnegie-Mellon University, March 1987.

[5] DoD-STD-2167, *Defense System Software Development*, Department of Defense Military Standard, 4 June 85.

[6] P. Ward, *Structured Development for Real-Time Systems*. Englewood Cliffs, NJ: Prentice-Hall, 1986.

An Industrial Course in Software Quality Assurance

R B Hunter

Department of Computer Science, University of Strathclyde, Glasgow,
Scotland

ABSTRACT

An account of a course in Software Quality Assurance given to
industrial Software Engineers in Central Scotland. The University of
Strathclyde, in partnership with ten Information Technology Companies,
is providing a range of such courses to update employees in IT industries. An accumulation of credits from such courses leads to a Masters
degree.

1. Introduction

The need for more specialists in Information Technology and for the regular updating
of existing specialists in the UK has been recognized (NEDO[1983], Butcher[1984]).
To meet the former need a number of MSc (conversion) courses in Information Technology have been set up for graduates of numerate disciplines in Science and
Engineering. One such course is the MSc in Software Engineering at the University of
Stirling (Budgen, Henderson and Rattray [1986]) which has a strong industrial component. The MSc in Information Technology Systems at the University of Strathclyde
is more broadly based and covers Computer Science, Electronics and Business Studies
in approximately 40/40/20 proportions.

The need to update existing employees in IT industries might be met in a number of
ways. For example:

a) courses given within the confine of the employees workplace by individuals chosen
for their expertise in particular areas.

b) sending employees on courses offered by commercial training organizations (of
which there are many).

c) specialized courses given by Universities or Polytechnics in collaboration with
industry.

The author has experience of a) through courses given at the National Engineering Laboratory in East Kilbride and at the Headquarters of the South of Scotland Electricity Board in Glasgow. b) is a very expensive option for companies based in Scotland to send staff to professionally marketed courses in London. Several Universities in the UK have set up joint schemes with industry partly to provide c). Examples are UNITE, associated with the University of Newcastle upon Tyne and the Information Technology Institute associated with the University of Salford in Manchester.

The Central Belt of Scotland (sometimes called Silicon Glen!) is well endowed with IT companies. Some are well established while others have arrived more recently with the help and encouragement of the Scottish Development Agency's Locate in Scotland initiative. Many of these latter companies have their headquarters abroad in the USA or Japan. A profile of the IT companies in the central belt of Scotland would show the following features:

1) Many of the companies have hardware as well as software interests.

2) Some of the companies are defense contractors.

3) There is an interest in developing real-time software.

4) There are at present, few large Software Houses, though this is beginning to change.

Many of the companies are situated relatively close to Glasgow, therefore commuting daily to Strathclyde University to attend courses is feasible for most employees. The University has contacts in many of the companies through former students, and collaborative research and consultancy are already taking place.

2. ITACS

The University of Strathclyde entered in to partnership with ten locally based IT companies in 1986 to form the Information Technology Associate Companies Scheme (ITACS) which has the following primary objectives:

To establish a close working relationship between the associate companies and the University to improve the quality and relevance of education and training in IT.

To retrain the staff of associate companies by means of modular courses which are capable of leading to higher qualifications.

To promote an increase in the number of postgraduates in the IT field.

To effect a general improvement in access to students by companies and to the University by company staff.

The Scheme is managed by the ITACS Management Committee comprising five representatives of the University plus the Technical and Course Managers of the scheme. This committee in turn receives guidance from an Industrial Advisory Board comprising one representative from each company. The scheme is financed partly by the companies themselves and partly by the Scottish Development Agency. It was envisaged that this partnership will give rise to various forms of collaboration such as consultancy, joint projects etc.

The courses offered under the scheme cover most aspects of Information Technology including Software Engineering, Electronics and Office Automation and are open to companies outside ITACS as long as places are available. The courses are intended to be of high quality held in purpose built accommodation and taught by experts in the field. Students attending courses have the use of Hewlett Packard Unix based workstations and all courses have a strong practical emphasis. Each course lasts four or five consecutive days. It was decided at an early stage that it was preferable from the companies point of view to release employees in blocks of this size rather than for one or two half days per week over a longer period. In this paper we look at the range of courses in the area of Software Engineering and particularly at the ITACS course in Software Quality Assurance.

3. Courses in Software Engineering

There are four courses in the Software Engineering area. These are:

Software Design Methodologies
Systems Analysis
Systems Design
Software Quality Assurance

The curricula for the courses were designed jointly with the industrial partners and between them, the four courses cover most of what is normally considered as Software Engineering with minimal overlap between the courses. It was realized at an early stage, that no assumptions could be made about the order in which students would attend the various courses. This would depend too much on the ability of companies to release employees during particular weeks of the year, the expertise that the company required at a particular time and so on. For example, the SQA course is taken by students who have already attended other Software Engineering courses and by students who have attended none of the other Software Engineering courses and may never attend any of them. Although this seemed to be a problem at the start, further thought suggested that as long as some background material was included at the start of each course, it would be possible for each course to stand on its own.

4. Students' background

As far as the SQA course is concerned, and other Software Engineering Courses appear to be similar, students may be divided into three major categories:

1) Practising Software Engineers who had completed their formal education ten or more years previously.

2) Employees who, although established in the IT industry for some time, had moved in to software recently from some other area (usually electronics). This is presumably because some of the companies have become more involved in software than hitherto.

3) Recent graduates in an IT related area who wished to specialize in Software Engineering or more specifically in SQA.

We felt it was important to emphasize the major SQA issues for all three groups. Some of the first group were already working in SQA and all of them were active in some aspect of Software Engineering. In general, they were fairly up-to-date with the precise area in which they were working, but their knowledge of related areas was often patchy and sometimes dated. The SQA course was not really designed for the second group, but due to a shortage of Software Engineers, this group is likely to occupy about 10% of the places on these courses. These students were being exposed to most of the course material for the first time and it was important not to submerge them in too much detail. The third group was the most up-to-date in formal education, and had often attended other ITACS courses in the recent past or would be doing so the near future. They expected to be given a clear view of how SQA fitted in with related areas.

Fairley [1987] has argued that Master's level courses in Software Engineering are best appreciated by students with a knowledge of the industry and most of our students were in this category. The Master of Software Engineering program at Seattle University is also designed for students who already have some experience of the software engineering industry (Mills[1987]).

Each student group made contributions to the course. In particular, the software engineers were able to give first hand accounts of their experiences (good and bad) of producing quality software. It was important for the success of the course to get to know the students individually, and to understand their various backgrounds. From this point of view, there would be some merit in holding the courses on company sites as was suggested by one of the participants. As it was, informal contact was possible during coffee breaks and lunchtime as well as during tutorials and practical sessions.

5. SQA Course

The content of the SQA course was influenced by the backgrounds of the attendees, the work being done by the companies and, to an extent, the interests of the Computer Science Department giving the course.

At the time the course was first offered (summer 1987) there was considerable interest in SQA being shown by most of the Associate Companies. Most of them had identified the SQA function and had already or were about to commit resources to SQA. Some had recently appointed SQA staff and some of these people attended the first course. It is probably fair to say that some of the companies and some of the SQA staff were not entirely clear about the role of SQA in the software production process and it was therefore more important to try and clarify this role rather than describe detailed techniques. Thus the SEI curriculum module in this area (Brown [1987]) was not covered in all its detail, though some of its excellent practical exercises could have been used for tutorial purposes. As already pointed out, we were also unable to assume that the students had the prerequisite knowledge required by the SEI course.

The four day course naturally divided itself in to four sections the syllabi of which are given in the Appendix.

> Software Development Process
> Software Production
> Software Evaluation
> Case Study

5.1. Software Development Process

The idea of a Software Development Process was introduced via the traditional Software Lifecycle with which most of the students were familiar. The concepts of formal/informal processes and mature/immature processes were introduced. How SQA may be built in to the process and the roles of SQA teams, SQA plans and SQA Standards were also introduced.

At this stage we emphasized that the quality of delivered software is critically dependent on the development process(es) used in construction, and that well- defined processes led to consistent results. SQA consists of ensuring that well-defined practices are followed throughout the software development process and also of monitoring the subprocesses involved from a quality viewpoint.

While the need for SQA is acknowledged in the Software Industry, there is confusion as to what its role should be. Analogies with other industries are frequently made, but can be overstretched. A proper introduction to SQA should ensure that a constructive view of quality assurance is put over and should also lead to a better understanding of the Software Development Process itself.

5.2. Software Production

In order to understand the role of SQA, it is necessary to look at the procedures in the development process which are critically involved in the production of quality software. Some of the procedures (planning, monitoring progress and configuration management for example) are managerial. As far as possible these management functions should be integrated with the technical functions using the same tools and databases where appropriate.

On the technical side, the principal issues raised in this section were:

1) Software Requirements - what is required? - checking for completeness and consistency - traceability.

2) Software Design - formal and informal methods. Simple examples of formal specifications/designs. (informal methods are treated in other courses). Verification.

3) Programming standards, choice of language.

4) Walkthroughs - how they are organized, reviews and audits.

5) Static checkers and other automated tools.

Some of the issues which arose informally during this section were:

Is there a conflict between the role of the software manager and that of the SQA team?

Are formal specifications intelligible?

How should walkthoughs be conducted? Who should attend them?

Is the cost of SQA justified?

Discussion of these issues reinforced the view that SQA is not an exact science. There is clearly more than one way of doing it. However most people were at least convinced that doing it was better than not doing it at all. Discussing SQA seemed to raise questions on many aspects of current practices in the area of software development.

5.3. Software Evaluation

This section was introduced by discussing the desirable 'qualities' of software and its measurable aspects. The ideas of derived and process metrics were thus introduced and the possibility of relating the two types of metrics by means of a mathematical model. Process metrics discussed included Halstead's and McCabe's metrics as well as dataflow and call graph metrics.

A discussion on software testing emphasized the two roles of testing

a) to find errors

b) to measure quality

As far as a) was concerned black box and glass box methods were described as was the role of test plans and test paths. The ultimate aim of b) is to be able to ensure that software is sold with a guarantee as to its quality. Superficially this has much in common with quality control in other industries but again the analogy can be stretched too far. The idea of statistical sampling in the manufacturing industries is well understood but there is nothing which *exactly* corresponds to this in software production. Statistical testing investigates the behaviour of the software with different input data, and can be used in the certification process along with data collected throughout the software development process which measure conformance with the predefined process etc. These ideas are discussed and although product certification is viewed as being beyond the state of the art at present, the problems which it highlights provide valuable insights into the role of SQA in the Software Development Process.

5.4. Case Study

A presentation on the IBM Clean Room approach to Software Development brought together a number of ideas already discussed, including the use of formal methods, unit testing and statistical testing. It also allowed the students the opportunity to comment on aspects of the Software Development Environments found in their companies and to relate their own work to some of the SQA issues.

5. Practical Work

So far we have not allocated a large amount of time to practical work on the SQA course (about 2*2hours) and this time has been devoted to gaining experience of using SQA tools. A single tool, Qualigraph(Szentes and Gras[1986]) , has been used to give students an opportunity to evaluate complexity metrics in software which has already been written, and also to identify test paths and test data for existing software.

Qualigraph can be used to calculate a wide range of source code metrics including Halstead and McCabes metrics and various data flow and call graph metrics as well as giving statistics on the use of various statement types. Experimentation with the system allowed students to gain an appreciation of the relative values of using various metrics and how they related to the programming methodology used, programming style, complexity of the problem and so on. They were also able to use the Qualigraph system to spot anomalies in programs and thereby (in some cases) correct errors. Qualigraph can be used with a wide range of source languages but so far students have only used Pascal. There could be some benefit in future of allowing students to use the language with which they are most familiar.

In the second practical session students used Qualigraph to identify test paths in a program supplied to them. From these test paths they were then able to suggest suitable test data for the program concerned and to perform glass box testing with this data.

5.6. Student Feedback

Feedback from the students attending the course was obtained in a number of ways

1) from an open discussion session at the end of the course.

2) from a questionnaire completed by each student after the course was finished and returned via the ITACS manager.

3) at a follow-up day held several weeks after the end of the course.

Some of the comments received were

that SQA is worth investing in

that formal methods are impractical

that source code metrics are/are not useful

that software engineers need to keep up with the state of the art

There were also comments on the domestic arrangements and the suggestion was made that some of us should vary our lecturing style from that used to undergraduates. Clearly we will have to think about this one!

There was no doubt that the course had been stimulating. For a course intended as Continuing Education rather than Training for Software Engineers we considered it more important to have raised a lot of questions than to have provided all of the answers.

6. Conclusions

Our experience of developing and presenting the SQA course in the context of ITACS suggest that

1) The course should leave the students with a clear understanding of the main issues in SQA.

2) Practical work is important even in a topic which does not obviously lend itself to practical work.

3) Students' own experiences provide a valuable input to the course.

4) Case studies help to put the issues in perspective.

5) An appropriate teaching style is required for these courses.

Acknowledgements

Professor R H Thayer of California State University at Sacramento acted as guest lecturer on the first SQA course and many of the ideas in this paper were inspired by his contribution to that course. The contributions of colleagues who have assisted with subsequent courses is also acknowledged.

References

Brown B J[1987], Assurance of Software Quality, Curriculum Module SEI-CM-7-1.0(preliminary), Carnegie Mellon University, Software Engineering Institute, 1987.

Budgen D, Henderson P, Rattray C[1987], Academic/Industrial Collaboration in a Postgraduate Master of Science Degree in Software Engineering, Software Engineering Education, The Educational Needs of the Software Community edited by Gibbs N E and Fairley R E, Springer-Verlag, 1987.

Butcher[1984], IT Skills Shortages Committee chairman John Butcher MP, Department of Trade and Industry, 1984.

Fairley R E[1987], Software Engineering Education - An Idealized Scenario, Software Engineering Education, The Educational Needs of the Software Community, edited by Gibbs N E and Fairley N E, Springer Verlag, 1987.

Mills E E[1987], The Master of Software Engineering Program at Seattle University after six years, Software Engineering Education, The Educational Needs of the Software Community edited by Gibbs N E and Fairley R E, Springer-Verlag, 1987.

Mills H D, Dyer M and Linger R C[1987], Cleanroom Software Engineering, IEEE Software, 1987.

NEDO[1983], Crisis in UK IT, NEDO Report, 1983.

Szentes J and Gras J[1986], Some Practical Views of Software Complexity Metrics and a Universal Measurement Tool, First Australian Software Engineering Conference, 1986.

Appendix

SQA Syllabus

Software Development Process
The Software Life Cycle - Waterfall, spiral and other models.
Formal and informal processes, mature and immature processes.
Definition of SQA.
SQA plans, SQA standards, SQA teams.

Software Production
Managerial and Technical Processes (and their integration).
Requirements and Traceability.
Configuration management.
Choice of Language.
Formal specification and verification.
Walkthroughs, audits and reviews.
Automated tools.

Software evaluation.
Quality characteristics - reliability, testability etc.
Source code and other metrics.
Process metrics.
Testing, black box and glass box, test plans.
Statistical testing, modeling and certification.
Compiler validation.

Case Study
IBM Clean Room - an informal/formal approach to verification coupled with
unit testing and statistical testing.

SEI Report:
The Design of an MSE Curriculum

Mark A. Ardis
Software Engineering Institute
Carnegie Mellon University

ABSTRACT

Six required courses for a Master of Software Engineering (MSE) program are described:

- Software Systems Engineering
- Specification of Software Systems
- Principles and Applications of Software Design
- Software Generation and Regeneration
- Software Verification and Validation
- Software Project Management

For each course, a detailed list of topics and subtopics is given, with educational objectives noted. Principal references, suggested exercises, and other teaching concerns are discussed for each course.

These courses were designed by a group of educators at a recent workshop held at the Software Engineering Institute. An attempt was made to cover all of the software engineering topics and educational objectives described in [Ford 87][1] (a report on previous efforts toward describing an MSE program). This report is termed a *design*, because:

- it is a more detailed description than the *specification* [Ford 87],
- it was reviewed for internal consistency and verified for agreement with the specification,
- it provides sufficient detail to allow independent *implementation* by instructors.

The design process is also described.

---

[1] Ford, Gary, Norman Gibbs, and James Tomayko, *Software Engineering Education: An Interim Report from the Software Engineering Institute*, Technical Report CMU/SEI-87-TR-8, Software Engineering Institute, Carnegie Mellon University, Pittsburgh, Pa., 1987

The Software Engineering Graduate Program at the Boston University College of Engineering

John Brackett, Thomas Kincaid and Richard Vidale
Department of Electrical, Computer and Systems Engineering
College of Engineering, Boston University

The College of Engineering has developed a Master's degree program in software engineering to meet the needs of industrial software development and management. The program will educate software engineers by providing courses in the technology, methodology and management of software development. The program incorporates the best features of the Master of Software Engineering curriculum formerly offered at the Wang Institute of Graduate Studies [1,2] and the MS in Systems Engineering, Software Engineering Option, offered at Boston University. A doctoral program leading to the Ph.D. in Engineering, with research specialization in software engineering, is also available in the College of Engineering.

The software engineering Master's program is offered in the Department of Electrical, Computer and Systems Engineering as the Software Engineering Option of Master of Science in Systems Engineering; the program is expected to be renamed the Master of Science in Software Systems Engineering by the fall of 1989. The program emphasizes the understanding of both hardware and software issues in the design and implementation of software systems. Special emphasis is placed on the software engineering of two important classes of computer systems: embedded systems and networked systems. Ada is the language used in a majority of the courses.

Both full- and part-time programs are available, and a majority of the program will be available on television for those corporate locations which are members of the Boston University Corporate Classroom interactive television system. The program may be completed in twelve months by full-time students.

I. Curriculum

The master's program requires the completion of nine four-credit semester-length courses: six required courses, two technical electives, and a team project. There are two entrance tracks: one for those with a hardware background (Electrical or Computer Engineering) and another for those with a software background (Computer Science or work experience in software development).

The required courses common to both tracks are:

> Applications of Formal Methods
> Software Project Management
> Software System Design
> Computer as System Component
> Software Engineering Project

Those students with a hardware-oriented background take the sequence:

Advanced Data Structures
Operating Systems

Those students with a software-oriented background take the sequence

Switching Theory and Logic Design
Computer Architecture

The objective of the two sequences is to provide each group of students with material lacking in their background. The computer engineering program in the College of Engineering provides the basis for the hardware-oriented aspects of the program.

The prerequisite structure of the program is shown in Figures 1 and 2; the catalog description of the courses are included in the Appendix. The technical electives may be selected from courses in the areas of software engineering, computer engineering and computer science.

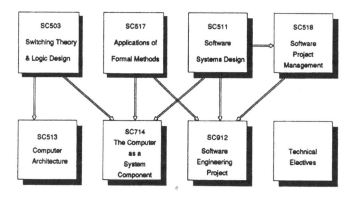

Figure 1: Prerequisite Structure, Software Background

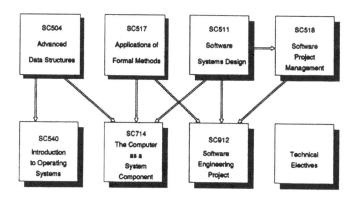

Figure 2: Prerequisite Structure, Hardware Background

The capstone software development project is performed by teams of students during a single semester. The project is designed to integrate and apply the knowledge acquired in the program, and emphasizes team techniques, communication skills, and planning. Projects are judged by both academic and industrial standards, and are closely supervised by a faculty member.

II. Admission Requirements

The minimum admission requirements to the program are:

> BS from accredited institution, with at least a B average
> Programming experience in:
> > a block structured, high level language
> > an assembly language

Courses in discrete mathematics, probability and statistics, and data structures are recommended, but are not required for admission. However, students without this background, which may be gained either through courses or work experience, may be required to complete remedial material or courses before beginning the program. Successful work experience in software development is preferred, but not required.

The College plans to restrict enrollment in the program to 60 full-time equivalent degree candidates. Since many of the students will be part-time students, 125-150 students are expected to be masters degree candidates by the 1990-91 academic year. The enrollment in the degree program in the 1988 spring semester was approximately 20, plus those students who were taking courses in the program as a non degree candidates. Many of these special students are expected to become degree candidates.

III. Cooperation with Industry

The College of Engineering has given a high priority to the strengthening of ties with companies involved in software development. The curriculum has been designed, with significant industrial input, to meet the needs of industry for students trained in both the technical and management aspects of software engineering. The College has formed an Industrial Advisory Board, comprised of technical leaders from major Boston-area companies, to advise the Dean and the faculty on the program's development.

In the Boston area there is a high demand for software engineers experienced in the development of software for computers which are components of larger systems. Although many of the job openings involve embedded systems for the Department of Defense, there are also many companies developing computer-based products for a diverse range of commercial applications. Therefore, the program is designed to educate software engineers who can develop high-quality software that works closely with a product's hardware.

In addition to the professional Masters program, the College is expanding its software-oriented research activities. Ph.D. level research in software engineering is expected to become an important part of the College's research activities during the next few years. The University recognizes that rapid advances in software engineering during the last decade have been spurred by research conducted in both academic and industrial settings. Therefore an important goal of the College is to forge effective technology transfer paths between the academic and industrial software research communities.

IV. Television-Based Instruction

In response to industrial requests, Boston University has given high priority to meeting the needs of students who can take only one or two courses a semester. The College of Engineering developed the Corporate Classroom interactive television system, beginning in 1983, in order to meet the needs of part-time students that can not easily commute to the main Boston University campus.

Courses are transmitted live from classrooms on campus. Off-campus students may ask questions by telephone. Student questions in the classroom can be heard by students in the television audience, and telephone questions are amplified so they can be heard in the classroom. Nearly all the courses are broadcast during the day, and most companies participating in the program give employees release time to view classes. Video tapes are available if a student misses a class or for review purposes. A courier takes materials to each corporate site and collects homework and project deliverables from the students. A student can attend on-campus classes, and instructors are available during specific hours by telephone for individual consultation. All exams are taken with the on-campus students. Many faculty meet personally with the students to review project work.

Five of the six required classroom courses in the software engineering masters program will be telecast; the exception is "The Computer as System Component" which will require use of the on-campus Embedded System Laboratory. In addition, a selection of elective courses will be available on television. Therefore, a student who carefully selects electives may complete seven of the nine courses required for the degree on television, and will need to come to campus for only two courses, the project course and "The Computer as a System Component."

Interest in taking the software engineering program on television is surprisingly high among students with management responsibility. For example, two of the best students in one of the authors' software requirements definition class in the fall of 1987 were managers with 35 and 100 people in their organization. These managers said television was the only way they could have taken the course, since their responsibilities made travel to the campus impossible. Both of them used video tapes extensively to make up for classes missed during business travel. When they did watch the class live, they asked some of the most penetrating questions.

Some important issues related to teaching software engineering on television have yet to be resolved. Students must be encouraged to form teams to work on projects, even if it means traveling to another site. Because some students are from locations where visitors are not allowed outside of normal working hours, team project work is hard to arrange. However, we believe it is a vital part of the program. One possible approach, as yet untried, is to provide meeting and computer facilities at least one Boston University suburban campus location.

The most important issue to be resolved is how to provide students with state of the art software engineering tools to support their course work. The television courses have traditionally relied upon dial-up access to computers on the main campus. However, with the increased importance of graphically-oriented tools on powerful personal computers and workstations, the software engineering program should not restrict the tools used in courses to those that are available via character-oriented terminals on

1200 baud telephone lines. The most obvious solution would be to request the companies sponsoring students to provide a "standard" workstation and a set of specified software tools. Since some of the sponsor companies manufacture workstations, this solution is not practical. The most feasible solution appears be to specify a set of software tools that are available on several hardware platforms and request that the sponsoring companies provide them to their students. We expect the members of the Industrial Advisory Board will need to focus attention in their organizations on how to have state of the art tools readily available to their students.

V. Program History

The Software Engineering Option in the Systems Engineering Master's program was approved by the College of Engineering faculty in the spring of 1980. The first degree was granted in 1982. The program enjoyed a slow, but steady, growth until sixteen students were matriculated in the spring of 1987. Following the acquisition of the Wang Institute by Boston University, Digital Equipment Corporation requested that the university seriously consider a major expansion of the existing College of Engineering program. During the early summer of 1987 the College faculty and administration prepared a proposal for the companies that had sponsored students at the Wang Institute. In July 1987 DEC agreed to provide a leadership grant to expedite the establishment of the expanded program. The acquisition of the software engineering library of the Wang Institute has given the College's students and faculty access to an excellent collection of software engineering materials.

The revised curriculum was approved by the College faculty in October 1987 and introduced in January 1988; it retains the original program emphasis on understanding both hardware and software issues in the design and implementation of software systems. The revised program incorporates major elements of the Master of Software Engineering curriculum formerly offered at the Wang Institute. 4 of the 8 required courses were presented in the spring of 1988; all of the required courses will be offered during the 1988-89 academic year.

VI. Comparison with the Wang Institute MSE Program

It is impossible to briefly compare the Wang Institute Master of Software Engineering program with the current College of Engineering program. However, it is useful to state three major differences between the two programs:

1. The WI program was oriented toward the software engineering of system software, such as operating systems and compilers, and stand alone software products. The BU program is oriented toward software systems that are an integral component of a larger system.

2. The WI program was designed for full-time students and part-time students who could obtain company release time to travel to the Tyngsboro campus during the work day. The BU program uses television to reach part-time students in their company and over a wider geographical area than was served by the WI.

3. The WI program required a minimum of one year of related work experience; the BU program has no work experience requirement. However, we expect the work experience of degree candidates to be, on the average, approximately equal.

VII. Future Challenges and Directions

The limiting factor in the growth of the program is the ability to recruit qualified faculty. Recruiting faculty with the required academic credentials and experience in software engineering is very difficult, and the emphasis in the program on hardware and systems issues makes the job even harder. We anticipate that some of the additional faculty will have a computer engineering background, with significant experience in software development.

A significant number of full-time Masters and Ph.D. students is essential to a high quality graduate program. These students, many of whom will be company sponsored and able to attend any one of the top research universities, must be actively recruited.

The corporate supporters of the program are already requesting that our courses be available by television to sites outside the current 40 mile signal range. Live satellite transmission of our courses is obviously feasible, and the College may test it at pilot sites during the 1988-89 academic year. However, an important part of the pilot program will be to investigate techniques, such as two-way video conferencing, that will allow a faculty member to review student project work remotely.

During the past year the College of Engineering has taken major steps to expand its activities in software engineering education. The current College of Engineering program owes a great deal to the pioneering work in software engineering education done at the Wang Institute. The curriculum developed at the Wang Institute has greatly influenced the content of the revised program. In addition, the 130 Wang Institute MSE graduates have demonstrated to their companies the value of graduate education in the field. Many of these graduates have been strong advocates of financial support from industry to preserve a software engineering program in the Boston area.

Dr. Wang recognized the need for industrially-oriented, high quality graduate education in software engineering long before most of his peers. Now that there is a wider perception of the need, we are confident that a long term university-industrial partnership can build a nationally recognized graduate program in software engineering at Boston University.

Bibliography

[1] M. Ardis, *Evolution of the Wang Institute Master of Software Engineering Program.* IEEE Transactions on Software Engineering, November, 1987.

[2] S. Gerhart, *Skills versus Knowledge in Software Engineering Education: A Retrospective on the Wang Institute MSE Program.* in Software Engineering Education: The Educational Needs of the Software Community, Springer-Verlag, 1987.

Description of Required Courses

SC503 - Switching Theory and Logic Design   (software background track only)

Analysis and synthesis of digital circuits including basic design techniques. Boolean algebra, switching functions, sequential machines. Characteristics of switching, memory, and input/output devices. Digital integrated-circuit families. Large-scale integration. Design of complex digital systems.

SC504 - Advanced Data Structures   (hardware background track only)

Review of basic data structures. Data structure support in machine architectures and high-level languages. Data abstraction and its implementation in different languages. Data structures for distributed systems and database design; multi-access data bases and structural support for transaction processing.

SC511 - Software Systems Design

Concept of the software product life cycle; various forms of a software product from requirements definition through operation and maintenance. Life cycle models and the activities performed in each phase. Requirements definition. Design concepts and design strategies. Role of rapid prototyping in requirements analysis and design. Analysis and design validation. Small team projects involving architectural and detailed design, implementation, testing, and modification.

SC513 - Computer Architecture   (software background track only)

The concepts of computer architecture. The von Neumann architecture and its critique. The semantic gap and approaches to its reduction. Object oriented architecture; the Intel iAPX432 system. The RISC architecture. High-level Language (HLL) architecture. The dynamic and flexible architecture. Parallel processing: pipelining, array processors, multiprocessors. Data flow architecture. Content-addressable memories, Distributed system architecture. Current trends in computer architecture research.

SC517 - Applications of Formal Methods

Formal foundations for the theory and practice of software engineering. Specification languages and verification techniques for showing an implementation is consistent with a specification. State transition and Petri net models of computation. Proofs of program properties; limitations of program testing. Fundamental techniques for the analysis of space and time complexity of algorithms. Applications of formal methods in a variety of system development contexts.

SC518 - Software Project Management

Planning, organization, staffing and control of a software project. Software project economics. Cost factors and cost estimation models. Cost/benefit tradeoffs, risk analysis. Project metrics for quality, schedule, budget and progress. Role of the project manager. Organization of the the development team. Case studies used to illustrate successes and failures in the management of actual projects.

SC540 - Introduction to Operating Systems   (hardware background track only)

Advanced study of real time systems and operating systems based on the framework of resource management. Emphasis on separating issues of mechanisms from policies.

SC714 - The Computer as a System Component

Systems engineering specifications of a computerized system. Distributed versus centralized computation. Design trade-offs in hardware and software development. Case studies of systems designed with embedded computers. Includes hands-on experience with the embedded systems laboratory

SC912 - Software Engineering Project

Projects may include some or all of the following activities: specification, design, implementation, testing and modification of a software system. The project is done in teams of students. The project course emphasizes team techniques, communication skills, planning, reporting, reviewing and documentation.

THE SOFTWARE ENGINEERING PROGRAMS
AT GEORGE MASON UNIVERSITY

Richard E. Fairley
Professor of Information Systems and Systems Engineering
School of Information Technology and Engineering
George Mason University
Fairfax, Virginia

INTRODUCTION

The Commonwealth of Virginia, through its Center for Innovative Technology, has provided funds to establish an academic program in software engineering at George Mason University. This paper describes our plans for the teaching, research, and technology transfer components of that program.

The program is housed in the School of Information Technology and Engineering at GMU. The School consists of four departments: Electrical and Computer Engineering; Computer Science; Operations Research and Applied Statistics; and Information Systems and Systems Engineering. In the School there are 3 undergraduate degree programs, five Masters programs, and one Ph.D. program in Information Technology which serves all four departments. The Master of Science in Software Systems Engineering degree program will be housed in the Department of Information Systems and Systems Engineering. Doctoral students in software engineering will utilize the existing Ph.D. program in Information Technology.

In addition to the four departments, the University has established a Center for Software and Systems Engineering within the School. The role of that Center as the research and technology transfer arm of the software engineering program is described below.

THE MASTERS PROGRAM

The Master of Science in Software Systems Engineering (MS-SWSE) program will consist of four core courses, four electives, and a two semester project or a six credit hour thesis, for a total of ten semester length courses of three credit hours each. The core courses are Introduction to Software Systems Engineering; Analysis, Prototyping, and Design; Formal Methods and Models in Software Engineering; and Software Project Management. A catalog description of each core course is provided in Table I.

A short list of permissible electives, from which each student will choose four, will be provided. Some elective courses are listed in Table II. It is anticipated that many of the elective courses will be offerings from other departments, and that many of the software engineering courses will provide desirable electives for other programs. Different sets of electives will be appropriate for students who plan to do technical work, to be managers, or to pursue doctoral studies. Most students will be encouraged to pursue the project option (working in teams) rather than a thesis and to work on group projects in the Center for Software and Systems Engineering.

Prerequisites for the MS-SWSE program include the following undergraduate courses or equivalent knowledge: structured programming in a modern programming language, data structures, discrete math, and assembly language/architecture. In addition, it is desired that students have two years of appropriate work experience in the software field upon matriculation.

Our plan for introducing the MS-SWSE program is to first offer the four core courses in Fall Semester, 1988. Both Systems Engineering and Computer Science will cross-list these courses and make them available to their Masters students who wish to specialize in software engineering. Students in each department will take the usual core requirements in their respective programs plus the four core courses and a project course in software engineering as the elective courses in their programs. In general, a rich interconnection of course sharing is anticipated among the various departments and programs in the School.

Work toward approval of the MS-SWSE degree will progress during the 1988-89 academic year. We anticipate approval by the Fall Semester, 1989.

THE CERTIFICATE PROGRAM

Individuals who have a Masters degree in a scientific or technical discipline from an accredited university are eligible for the Certificate Program in software systems engineering. Each applicant must also have the prerequisites for the MS-SWSE program (i.e., structured programming, data structures, discrete math, assembly language, and two years work experience). In order to obtain the Certificate, students must complete the four core courses and a one semester project course, for a total of 15 semester credits of graduate study.
The Certificate program is thus a post-Masters program that corresponds to roughly one-half of a Masters program in software engineering. We anticipate that the Certificate program will be attractive to those who are trained in other disciplines and who now find that their work is primarily in software engineering.

THE PH.D. PROGRAM

The existing Ph.D. program in Information Technology serves as the single doctoral program for all students in the School. Doctoral students complete a set of breadth courses from the various departments in the School and, following successful completion of qualifying examinations, specialize in their chosen fields of endeavor. Each student is required to take a minimum of 24 credits of course work beyond the Masters program. Doctoral courses in software engineering to be introduced in the next one to three years are listed in Table III.

RESEARCH AND TECHNOLOGY TRANSFER PLANS

The Center for Software and Systems Engineering is the research and technology transfer component of the software engineering program at George Mason University. The overall goal for the Center is to develop innovations in software technology and diffuse those innovations into industry, governmental agencies, and educational institutions. In order to achieve this goal, the Center will conduct research into innovative methods, tools, and techniques that will shift the production and modification of computing software from a labor intensive endeavor to a technology intensive endeavor, thereby improving the productivity of software engineers and the quality of the software produced by those engineers.

Three fundamental keys to higher quality and increased productivity in software engineering are (1) better education and training for software engineers, (2) better software tools to support software engineering processes, and (3) an active effort to transfer knowledge and technology into industrial practice. These fundamental issues will be addressed by the Certificate program, Masters program, and Ph.D. program in software engineering, by coupling those programs to the activities of the Center, and by focusing our research efforts on innovations in software tools that support the methods and techniques of software engineering.
After an initial start-up period, the Center will be supported entirely by industry. Two types of industrial support are envisioned: subscription support at a given level per year, and support for projects of particular interest to a given company on a project-by-project basis.

Companies participating in subscription support will guide the ongoing research activities in the Center through their membership on a Center Advisory Board. In addition to guiding the research activities of the Center, these companies will enjoy several special benefits, including early access to the results produced by the Center, exclusive participation in regularly scheduled Center colloquia and seminars, and a guaranteed number of admission slots for their qualified employees to the Masters program in software engineering and Ph.D. program in information technology.

Employees enrolled in the Masters or Ph.D. program under this arrangement will have the opportunity to work in the Center under the supervision of Center faculty members on projects of special interest to their sponsors. One degree option will allow a corporate sponsored student on an 18 month assignment to the Center to complete course work requirements for the Masters degree in 9 to 12 months and spend the remaining 6 to 9 months working on a company sponsored project that fulfills the thesis or project requirements for the Masters degree. Ph.D. students might be assigned for longer periods of time to pursue dissertation research topics. Certificate studetns might be assigned for shorter periods of time. In addition, some companies may choose to assign personnel to the Center who are not pursuing a degree. This option will be available on a case-by-case basis.

The Center will also focus on knowledge transfer and technology transfer in software engineering. A goal of the Center is to shorten the typical 10 to 15 year time lag between development of a new approach in software engineering and adoption of that approach by industry.

Knowledge transfer will be a major goal of the Center. Several mechanisms are envisioned for dissemination of our work. The usual vehicles of technical reports, journal papers, and conference participation will be utilized. In addition, some innovative mechanisms are being investigated, including special two and three day in-depth workshops and research seminars on topics of interest to the sponsors; microwave and video transmission of seminars, short courses, and semester length courses to our industrial sponsors; hosting of visiting faculty members from other universities; and service as a clearinghouse on software engineering technology.

Experience has shown that the most effective knowledge transfer mechanism is to situate the people who have the desired knowledge in the organization seeking that knowledge. Our plan, described above, is to bring industry personnel into the Center, as graduate students working on topics of interest to their sponsors and as non-degree assignees on limited term assignments. These people will then carry the methods, tools, and techniques acquired during their stay within the Center back to their companies. In addition, it may sometimes be advantageous to have Center personnel spend a portion of their time working on projects within the sponsoring companies. The two way flow of personnel between the Center and the sponsors, particularly when coupled to the Masters and Ph.D. programs, will provide an extremely effective mechanism for knowledge transfer and technology transfer.

SUMMARY

This paper has presented plans for software engineering programs in the School of Information Technology and Engineering at George Mason University. Those plans include a Masters program in Software Systems Engineering, cross-listing of core courses in software engineering with Computer Science and Systems Engineering, a post-Masters Certificate program, development of doctoral level courses for the existing Ph.D. program in information technology, and evolution of the Center for Software and Systems Engineering into an industrially supported center for research and technology transfer in software engineering methods, tools, and techniques.

The Masters core courses, the Certificate program, and some of the Ph.D. courses will be introduced during the 1988-89 academic year. Several additional courses in software engineering will be introduced during the next one to three years. Approval of the Masters degree program is anticipated by Fall Semester of 1989. Industrial support for the Center for Software and Systems Engineering is expected to reach steady state within five years.

The overall goal for these plans is to evolve a center of excellence in software engineering within the School of Information Technology and Engineering at George Mason University that can serve the needs of high technology industries, governmental agencies, and educational institutions within the Commonwealth of Virginia and throughout the region.

TABLE I

Catalog Descriptions of Core Courses

INTRODUCTION TO SOFTWARE SYSTEMS ENGINEERING (3:3:0).
Prereq: Admission to the MS-SWSE program or permission of instructor. The software product lifecycle. Process models and metrics. Modern language concepts, including information hiding, inheritance, message passing, and concurrency as exemplified by Ada, Smalltalk, and other modern programming languages. Design, implementation, and validation of software systems using modern programming languages. Computer based tools to support modern software development practices are emphasized.

FORMAL METHODS AND MODELS IN SOFTWARE ENGINEERING (3:3:0).
Prereq: Admission to the MS-SWSE program or permission of the instructor. Formal mechanisms for specifying and verifying the correctness, reliability, and efficiency attributes of software systems. Elements of discrete mathematics. State transition, regular expression, context free, and applicative models. Assertions, Hoare axioms, and weakest preconditions. State machine, operational, and algebraic specification techniques. Key concepts from analysis of algorithms. Practical applications and computer based tools are emphasized.

REQUIREMENTS ANALYSIS, PROTOTYPING, AND DESIGN (3:3:0).
Prereq: Intro. to Software Systems Engr. or permission of the instructor. An in-depth study of methods, notations, documentation, and validation techniques for the analysis and design phases of software systems engineering. Topics include needs analysis, requirements specification, prototyping techniques, and design methods. Preparation and validation of requirements specifications, design documentation, test plans, and systems acceptance criteria are presented. Computer based tools for analysis, prototyping, and design of software systems are emphasized. Students will complete term projects that involve use of the methods presented in class.

SOFTWARE PROJECT MANAGEMENT (3:3:0).
Prereq: Intro. to Software Systems Engr. or permission of the instructor. Techniques for planning, staffing, monitoring, controlling, and leading a software project. Computer-based tools for planning and controlling software projects are emphasized, as are process models, configuration management, quality assurance, documentation plans, and metrics for measuring quality and productivity. In addition, leadership and team building skills for software engineering teams are emphasized. Students will work in teams of 3 or 4 to prepare case studies and to complete a group term project that involves development of a comprehensive project plan for a large scale software project. Written assignments and in-class presentations allow students to practice their communication skills.

TABLE II

SOME ELECTIVE COURSES IN THE MS-SWSE PROGRAM

- CASE Tools and Techniques
- Software Engineering Economics
- Software Quality Assurance
- Statistical Methods and Models
- Operating Systems
- Networks and Data Communications
- Introduction to Artificial Intelligence
- Microprocessors, Microcomputers, and Applications
- Modern Systems and Control Theory
- Elements of Systems Engineering
- Economic System Analysis
- Applied Statistics
- Operations Research I & II

TABLE III

SOME DOCTORAL LEVEL COURSES IN SOFTWARE ENGINEERING

- Software Productivity Analysis
- Software Prototyping Tools and Techniques
- Advanced Analysis & Design Methods
- Software Design for Real Time Systems
- Advanced Formal Methods and Models
- Statistical Methods for Software Engineering
- Metrics and Models in Software Engineering
- Software Reliability Models
- Software Engineering Environments
- Process Models for Software Engineering

Revised
Graduate
Software Engineering Curriculum
at
Monmouth College

Serafino Amoroso
Richard Kuntz
Thomas Wheeler
Bud Graff

Monmouth College
West Long Branch, New Jersey

Background

Monmouth College has been offering courses in Software Engineering at the graduate level for the past three years and two years ago began a fully accredited Master's program in Software Engineering. Two students completed the degree requirements during the summer of 1987, and it is expected that thirty students will complete the program of study during the summer of 1988. There are currently seventy-five students enrolled in the program; most of whom are part-time students taking from one to three courses each term. At the present time, 65% of the students are male, and the average age is twenty-five. All courses in the program are offered during the day and meet one day each week. Almost all the students are sponsored (Their tuition is fully paid, and they are granted release time to attend classes.) by local high technology firms. The list of participating organizations (those sponsoring five or more students) includes AT&T Bell Laboratories, AT&T Information Systems, Concurrent Computer Corporation, and Fort Monmouth.

A Software Engineering Curriculum Advisory Board, has assisted in the development and refinement of the curriculum and courses. The Board contains members from local high technology industries involved in the production of software. The current membership includes representatives from AT&T Bell Laboratories, AT&T Information Systems, Concurrent Computer Corporation, Fort Monmouth, Syntrex Corporation, Lakehust Naval Air Engineering Center, Lockhead Corporation, and Picatinny Arsenal. The Board meets twice a year to review and discuss the curricular issues concerning software engineering. Generally, it is concerned with theme and direction rather than with individual course syllabi. Considerable discussion has taken place relative to the system-engineering concepts of requirements and specifications and with the concept of computer communications and security. Because of the special interests and concerns of the local area, the revised program has special emphasis on those topics.

The Board also expressed considerable support for the team-project approach. It recognized the need to develop a library of large software systems case studies with supporting requirements, specifications, and configuration documentation. There is considerable difficulty in producing such material. The Board is continuing to look for ways to assist in the development and acquisition of such library materials.

As originally conceived, the program consisted of ten required courses. The courses were designed to cover four general areas: basic computer science, human factors, engineering principles, and computer communications. Throughout the curriculum, emphasis was placed on group projects and team solutions. Whenever feasible, course assignments were made on a group, project-team solution format. As a result of the first two years of experience, the program is undergoing major revision along several lines. Instead of a fixed program of study, more courses will be available, thus students will be able to tailor their program of study to better match their interests and needs. Although many of the original courses, being of fundamental importance, will continue to be a part of the program, the revised program has introduced a number of new and original courses (There will be two new courses on mathematical foundations, two courses that will present a different approach to teaching programming, a new laboratory course, and a very nontraditional course in principles of software engineering). This paper presents a rational for and a description of the revised program that is expected to be in effect by September.

The program is jointly sponsored by the Electronic Engineering Department and the Computer Science Department. A curriculum committee consisting of members from both departments reviews and monitors the curriculum; software engineering faculty hold joint appointments with one of the two departments designated as the home department for administrative purposes. It is anticipated that consideration will be given to providing separate department status to software engineering when the program reaches full enrollment objectives (50 FTE students) and full staffing.

Introduction

The term "Software Engineering" was coined around 1968 [1] to describe what was at the time a somewhat vaguely formulated approach to the solution of what was called "the software crisis." The "crisis" referred to the serious problems that were beginning to surface at the time concerned with the development of large software projects. The "problems"[2] can be summarized by: "The systems were delivered late." "The resulting systems did not meet customer expectations."

"They were far more costly than at first estimated." Finally, and perhaps most importantly, "The systems were very difficult to debug and to modify." (It was recognized then as inevitable that user requirements will change both during and after system development. This recognition is no less valid today). Although as practitioners, we continue to use the term "software engineering" for an organized, scientific approach to solving these problems, it was recognized even in 1968 that the software crisis is not concerned only with software. For example, the best engineered software is of little value if it does not satisfy the customer's requirements. Also, many of the partial solutions proposed were in fact methods of managerial control.

The Main Characteristics of the Program

The main emphasis of the Monmouth College Software Engineering Program as described in this paper will be on the engineering of software, but the topic is set in a larger, more encompassing framework, namely the engineering of large computer-systems. In addition to tradition software engineering, the program will cover selected topics from computer-systems engineering using a software engineering framework. The discipline of computer-systems engineering is strongly analogous to "architecture"in the traditional sense of the term but here is concerned with large computer-systems rather than with bridges and buildings. As with the traditional architect, the topics of requirements development, system specifications, system modeling, and system design will be central. The discipline of software engineering, on the other hand, is concerned with the more specific topic of crafting software products that will usually be components of the larger computer systems. As the traditional architect must also have a thorough understanding of the state-of-the-art in building materials and construction techniques, so the computer-systems architect must have a thorough understanding of computer-system development technology and of program development methodologies, even though this may not be the main everyday activity. The software developer, on the other hand, will benefit from exposure to additional topics such as formal specifications, and system design verification. These are more in the domain of the computer-system architect but can be expected to soon routinely impact the software development process.

The Distinguishing Characteristics of the Program

The characteristics that distinguish the revised program from the initial software engineering program at Monmouth and other computer related programs at Monmouth as well as in New Jersey, have been developed to implement the general themes described above. The main distinguishing characteristics are:

- an emphasis on the emerging scientific and mathematical foundations. (The stress on theory will require significant training in mathematics; the relevant courses have been developed and will become a part of the program.)

- a laboratory where practical applications will be studied. (The laboratory applications will be in the form of continuing projects that will stimulate ideas for the final projects that are required of the students. Laboratory participation will be required of the faculty as well. A paradigm for this concept is that of a "teaching hospital.")

- an emphasis on communication science and technology as it relates to computer systems. (A program emphasizing the engineering of computer systems should have at least one subject area of major emphasis. The program has several areas of specialization, listed below, but the main one will be communication science and technology, a critically important aspect of just about every large computer-system. Monmouth College is fortunate to have faculty with special expertise in this area and is located at the center of a major communications infrastructure. It is understandable that our industrial sponsors have a special interest in that topic as well.)

- a special sequence of courses on the Theory and Practice of Programming. (This is described below.)

- finally, a case studies and project-oriented approach throughout the curriculum. (This has been true with the program from the beginning, and it will continue.)

Program Description

Students entering the program are expected to have adequate preparation for a rigorous curriculum and to have specific expertise in computer science and mathematics that includes at a minimum, programming ability in a modern high-level language, a working knowledge of data structures and operating systems, and a reasonable degree of mathematical maturity, generally, those topics that are beginning to be found in the newly formed undergraduate course on discrete mathematics. Ideally, it is expected that the students are to be professional programmers, computer system engineers, or managers wishing to keep abreast of the latest developments in the profession by examining some of the newly emerging methods of system and program development as well as their underlying mathematical principles.

An important feature of the revised program is the identification of a core of required courses and the introduction of additional elective courses. Students are expected to complete six core courses and choose four others from a list of electives;

each course carries three credits. The courses in the core are intended to expose the student to the general basic material that constitutes the major themes of modern software engineering; in particular, through this selection of core courses, the student will gain requisite skills in the scientific and mathematical foundations of software engineering, principles and practices of software engineering, individual programming methodologies, computer communications and network theory, software engineering management practices, and human factors and social interactions through the laboratory practicum. A more detailed discussion of the core courses is found in the next section.

The program provides for individual student concentrations in areas of special interest. This is provided through the electives courses and through faculty guidance. At the present time, these areas of special interest are:

- Communication Systems and Communication Technology

- Programming Methodology

- Formal Specification and Verification

- Computer System Security

- System Requirements Engineering

- Management of Large Software Development Projects

- System Configuration and Management Technologies

The Program Courses

Core Courses:

SE 501 - Mathematical Foundations of Software Engineering I (new)

This course is being designed to help make more accessible to our students must of the relevant but more mathematical literature on such topics as program correctness proofs, formal specification techniques, and models of concurrent processes. The course will emphasize the notion of "proof," and of mathematics as a descriptive language. The course will include some of the fundamental concepts and results from the theory of automata and from formal logic, as well as an introduction to the notion of solvable and unsolvable decision problems.

SE 505 - Programming-in-the-large (new)

This course is concerned with the development of large programs, a process sometimes referred to an "multiperson programming." The topics covered will include abstract data types, modular design, interface specification, and concurrent programming techniques.

SE 508 - Project Management (new)

This course is concerned with the planning, staffing, and control of software development projects. It will discuss the integration of management techniques with the newly developing software engineering methodologies and software metrics. The course will discuss project cost estimation models, software contracts, annual statements, budgeting, and accountability. Social aspects of project management will also be covered, including human factors, group motivation, and behavior under stress.

SE 510 - Computer Networks (existing)

The course provides an introduction to telecommunication networks with a software engineering emphasis. The ISO protocol architecture is used as a reference, and algorithms that operate at each layer of the protocol hierarchy are described with emphasis on the physical data link and physical layers. The course includes a discussion of routing algorithms, queueing theory, circuit switching, packet switching, internet protocols, and integrated Service Digital Network, and CCITT No. 7.

SE 516 - Software Engineering (revised)

This course should be taken early in the program since it is intended to prepare the student for many of the courses to follow. It will introduce a variety of approaches and views on the central topics of system development "life-cycle models," "system prototyping," "system requirements development," "system specification," and "high-level system design." The topics will vary from very practical and immediately applicable to highly theoretical and philosophical. A quotation from [7] expresses what is the most important topic in this course, if not in the whole program. "The hardest single part of building a software system is deciding precisely what to build No other part of the conceptual work is as difficult as establishing the detailed technical requirements, including all the interfaces to people and machines, and to other software systems. No other part of the work so cripples the resulting system if done wrong. No other part is more difficult to rectify later." A similar remark from [3] will round out this comment. (Note that Tony Hoare uses the term "chief programmer" for our "computer-systems engineer.") The chief programmer, like the architect, will start by discussing requirements with his client. From education and experience, the programmer will be able to guide his client to an understanding of his true needs and avoidance of expensive feature of dubious or even negative value. From respect for the professional status of the programmer, the client will accept and welcome this guidance. This kind of mutual understanding and respect is essential to any relationship between a professional and his client or employer."

SE 525 - System Project Implementation (Laboratory Practicum) (existing)

The emphasis will be on group projects and on developing the skills needed for group interactions. The course will cover such topics as modularization, information hiding, module interface development, documentation, and semiformal system design verification. A system will be designed and documented by a team of about seven programmers. System projects under preparation, any one of which could be used here, include an office automation system, a message switching system, a communication protocol implementation, a text formatter, and a text editor.

Elective Courses:

SE 502 - Mathematical Foundations of Computer Science II (new)

The course covers predicate logic in some detail. Applications will be chosen to introduce the student to problem-solving techniques in artificial intelligence, and to the foundations of logic programming.

SE 506 - Programming-in-the-small (new)

This course will concentrate on programming done by an individual independently of any larger context. The course will discuss some (informal) ideas from "structured programming"[9], some less informal ideas on program development[10], and then a formal program development methodology based on correctness proofs. Most of the semester will be devoted to the latter topic[11],[12].

SE 511 - Protocol Engineering (revised)

This course will build on our Computer Networks course. It will emphasize concepts, issues and design trade-offs rather than descriptions of specific commercial or military protocols. The intimate relationship between protocol engineering and software engineering will be demonstrated throughout the course. The course will contain a discussion of formal mathematical techniques for describing and specifying protocols such as finite-state machines, extended finite-state machines, Petri nets, formal grammars, and language approaches such as Estelle, LOTOS, and SDL. The emerging techniques for automatic protocol specification, validation, verification, and implementation will also be discussed. Throughout the course, specific examples from the ISO and CCITT will be used as illustrative examples. An integral part of the course, students will design, specify, implement and test several protocols.

SE 540 - Selected Topics in Software Engineering (existing)

The contents of this course will vary with the interest of the lecturer. Initially, the course will concentrate on the topic of computer security. The lecture material will be based on the seminar material prepared for the National Security Agency by Dr. Rein Turn, and from material prepared by the SEI.

SE 509 - Programming Languages (existing)

Analysis of the underlying structure of high-level languages, including fourth generation languages and application generators. Existing languages are compared through subjective and objective measures. The principles and techniques of software engineering will be used to assess different languges and to highlight the importance of their features.

SE 514 - Computer Architecture (existing)

An integrated view of the logical design of a digital computer including hardware, firmware and operating system functions that affect software. Concepts such as CPU, control unit, microprocessing, bus contention and arbitration, interrupts, I/O handling and interfacing are covered.

SE 515 - Operating System Implementation (existing)

Fundamental operating system concepts - mutiprocessing, scheduling, deadlock, protection and relocation, virtual memory, security, and file systems. It covers principles of design decisions and design methodology, as will as policies and mechanisms. It focuses on the design and implementation of general-purpose multiprogramming systems for third and fourth generation architectures.

SE 519 - Database Management Systems (existing)

Theoretical and practical aspects of database managment systems and their appliations - hierarchical, network, and relational models for DBMS design, the issues of access, integrity, security and privacy, and maintenance for each model in various types of applications. Practical problems and design issues in database implementation will be discussed.

Finally, certain courses are under consideration and, although considered very important, have not been fully developed.

Program and System Development Environments:
AI and Expert Systems Technology,
Computer Graphics
Distributed Systems

Below is the curriculum chart for the proposed program. A student should take the courses in order of columns i.e. a new student taking only one course a term should follow the courses in the first column (First sequence) then in the second year should take the courses in the second column (Second sequence) etc. A student taking two courses a term should follow the first and second columns then in the second year should follow the third and fourth columns.

Software Engineering Curricula

	First Sequence	Second Sequence	Third Sequence	Fourth Sequence
Fall Semester	SE 501 Math Foundations	SE 516 Software Engineering I	SE 505 Programming in-the-large	SE 510 Network Design
Spring Semester	Elective Group A	SE 508 Project Management	Elective Group A or B	Elective Group A,B or C
Summer Semester		Elective Group A		SE 525 System Project Implementation

Group A: SE 502 Math Foundations II
                  SE 514 Computer Architecture
                  SE 519 Database Management
                  SE 509 Programming Languages

Group B: SE 506 Programming-in-the-small
                  SE 515 Operating System Implementation
                  SE 540 Special Topics

Group C: SE 511 Protocol Engineering

Long range plans include the development of a Ph.D. program that is built upon the foundations presented in computer science, electronic engineering, and software engineering. That program may be in any of the above areas or in a companion area such as computer systems engineering.

Acknowledgments

The inspiration and guidance for this program organization has come from sources. The writing of Tony Hoare[3], Edsgar Dijkstra[4], Harlan Mills[5], Fred Brooks[6], and last but by no means least, David Parnas[7], were particularly motivating. Among these references, the monograph "The Mythical Man-Month," and the paper "Programming is an Engineering Profession," are required reading in Software Engineering I. In fact, about half of the material in that course is based on the writings of David Parnas.

References

[1] The NATO Conference on Software Engineering, October 1968.

[2] These comments about the software crisis are quoted quite often. Our source was the "Institute for Defense Analyses, Science and Technology Division, Paper P-1046," dated October 1974, by David Fisher.

[3] All of Tony Hoare's papers should be mentioned here. Of particular relevance in the present context is: "Programming is an Engineering Profession," Oxford University Report, Programming Research Group, 1982.

[4] There is no one paper that can be referenced here. Everything that Dijkstra has written is motivation for what we are trying to accomplish.

[5] Much of the work of Mills will be incorporated in our program. The paper "Software Development." IEEE Trans on Software Engineering, December, 1976, is pertinent.

[6] We call the attention of reader to the classic: "The Mythical Man-Month," Addison-Wesley, 1974, and also to:

[7] "No Silver Bullet: Essence and Accidents of Software Engineering." IEEE Computer, April 1987.

[8] David Parnas has over the last twenty years written a great number of papers. For practical, immediately useful material, there is no better source of information on the topics of computer-system and software engineering. We will mention here only his lecture notes from his course "Applying Engineering Discipline to Software," Summer Institute in Computer Science, Wang Institute, 1985.

[9] A suitable source of material here is: "Structured Programming: Theory and Practice" by Linger, Mills, and Witt, Addison-Wesley, 1979.

[10] For this material, we have in mind: "Principles of Computer Programming: A Mathematical Approach" by Mills, Basili, Gannon, and Hamlet, Allyn and Bacon, 1987.

[11] "A Discipline of Programming" by Edsgar Dijkstra, Prentice-Hall, 1976.

[12] "The Science of Programming" by David Gries, Springer-Verlag, 1981.

Embedded Computer Systems

Requirements Analysis & Specification - An Industrial Course

Jonah Z. Lavi (Loeb), Michael Winokur
Israel Aircraft Industries
Ben Gurion Airport, Israel

ABSTRACT

IAI, Israel Aircraft Industries, has developed an industrial course to train its engineers in the analysis and specification of embedded computer systems (ESC) and their software. The course, based on a method which has been developed at IAI over the last eight years, blends known methods with original IAI developments. The approach stresses a total systems engineering view which considers the analysis of all systems aspects, not only the software. It discourages analysis of software alone without considering the entire system viewpoint. STATEMATE, a tool specially developed to support the method, is also introduced in the course.

The paper describes briefly the IAI method and the tool, the objectives of the course, its structure, contents and organization. That is followed by the lessons learned, future developments in the method and courses.

INTRODUCTION

Modern embedded computer systems are very complex. Many of them are multilevel systems including many computers in each level. Most of them are responding dynamically to random external signals and sequences of external events. Their dynamic behaviour depends also on the operational history of the system and on very complex logic conditions (WHIT84). Their analysis and specification requires a total systems approach considering all the aspects dictated by the application and the implementation: hardware, software, and communications.

Twenty to thirty percent of the system's development effort should be devoted to the analysis of the systems and to top level design, knowing that any mistakes made during this phase are very expensive to correct later on. This has been known for many years. In spite of this, in most projects this phase is handled inadequately, costing the companies fortunes in redesign and recoding of software.

It is easy to accuse engineers of not spending enough time and effort in systems analysis. Or, even worse, of not doing the analysis job adequately. There are however good reasons for the inadequate analysis of so many systems. Let us consider just a few of them. The complexity of the systems is tremendous. Relatively few people are trained in the analysis of such complex systems and very few have the necessary experience. Even the best engineers seldom do a systematic analysis since they were never taught how to do it.

People are not taught systems analysis methods because many believe that they cannot be taught. Others say that they do not know how to teach a good course in systems analysis and requirements specification. This statement was made for example by Al Pietrasanta (PIE186), of IBM, in response to a question when he described the IBM software engineering training program. Engineers also cannot learn the methods by themselves since no comprehensive literature is available. Furthermore, we feel that taking a course or reading a book is not sufficient. Inexperienced engineers have to be guided in the analysis of such projects by more experienced people after they have completed the necessary courses.

IAI faced this problem eight years ago. As a result we have studied the issues and have developed an embedded computer systems analysis and specification method. In the beginning we considered software requirements analysis alone. Soon we learned, however, that this is inadequete since most of the systems which we develop are multi - computer systems and we have to look at all systems aspects simultanously. We also learned very fast that you cannot separate the How's from the What's. In all practical projects you do top level design while preparing the specifications and both phases of the system development have to be handled almost simultaneously (BALZ82).

The IAI method has been forged by continuous cycles of work with projects, solutions of basic methodological problems, teaching of whatever we have learned and further development. The basic system specification and requirements analysis course to be described in this paper emerged from this cycle of work. It is being taught to our engineers and is updated at least four times a year. We expect that at the end of our basic course, which lasts five days, engineers will be able to analyze the specifications of a simple embedded computer system in terms of both its static and its dynamic characteristics, write a specification document and check its completeness.

During the initial steps in the development of the method we realized that you cannot expect engineers to prepare specifications of complex systems without the support of computerized tools. At the begining we used PSL/PSA (TIEC77). This tool does not support the dynamic aspects of the systems behaviour. We therefore had to sponsor the development of a new advanced tool supporting our method. The tool was developed, with our support and many of our ideas by AD-CAD, a subsidiary of i-Logix. It is known as STATEMATE (ILOG87). This tool is currently being used in all of our plants and is introduced during the basic course.

This paper describes the basic principles of our method which is taught in the course, the objectives of the course, its structure, contents and organization. We will conclude the paper with the lessons which we learned and review briefly our future plans for the development of the method and the course.

THE ANALYSIS METHOD

This part of the paper describes briefly the method taught in the course, the conceptual ECS (Embedded Computer Systems) model and basic techniques used in the analysis. The techniques described include: statecharts, functional decomposition, signal and data flow analysis methods and a suggested approach for the preparation of the resulting specififations. A more detailed description of the method is presented in other papers (LAVI84,LAVI86).

Basic Principles

The method taught is based on the following basic principles;

1. System, hardware and software aspects should be analyzed simultaneously during all of the analysis phases of the system and at all levels of system decomposition.

2. The functional (static) and the dynamic analyses of the systems should be carried out simultaneously in an iterative process.

3. It is impossible to separate the analysis phase and the resulting requirements specification phase from the top level system design phase. (BALZ82)

4. Known design templates of familiar systems and typical specifications of known types of subsystems should be used in the development and the analysis process. System or program families should be considered at the begining of the development of every new product (LOES85, PARN76).

5. The system should be analyzed using an abstract conceptual model of embedded computer systems that both systems and software engineers can understand.

The Conceptual Model of Embedded Computer Systems

The ECS conceptual model used in the development of the IAI method, is described in Figure 1. Using this model it is possible to describe any single or multicomputer system, single level or multilevel system, their software subsystems and modules. It is based on the assumption that they can be modelled and analyzed as hierachical control systems.

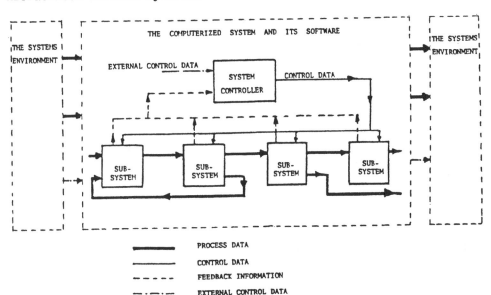

FIGURE 1 - THE BASIC SYSTEMS MODEL

Using this model, each system is decomposed into subsystems which carry out the system functions and a controller which controls their joint behaviour. Looking at the model, one realizes that it is necessary to analyze the relationships of the system with its environmental systems, e.g. the signals or data flows between them and the system. It is necessary to determine the subsystems and the data flows between them and to analyze the system control function or module which determines the overall operational behaviour of the system. Further, one has to determine the transfer functions of the subsystems. The model is described in detail by Lavi (LAVI84). It is not complete and will probably require some refinements and additions in the future. In this paper we will only summarize briefly the properties of the model.

The properties of the subsystems are;

1. They act jointly to achieve the system's objectives.

2. They can be either hardware, software or mixed hardware/software subsystems or modules.

3. They perform defined functions, with known characteristics and metrics.

4. Each one has a known transfer function which describes its static and dynamic behaviour.

5. Each one of them can be decomposed into subsystems and an internal controller.

The properties of the system controller are;

1. It controls the joint behaviour of the subsystems (modes and transitions between them, system configurations, activations of subsystem tasks and activities, etc.)

2. It can be centralized, distributed, synchronous, parallel, etc.

3. It is usually a multilevel controller implementing hierarchies of decisions.

4. Its major activities are described as a finite state machine.

5. It is possible to develop many controllers for the same group of subsystems (thus generating similar systems with different behaviours which can result in a family of systems (PARN76) or systems with many tops (MCFA82).

Figures 2 and 3 show an Automatic Teller Machine - ATM, an example used throughout our course. Figure 2 shows the system in its environment while Figure 3 shows the decomposition of the system into its subsystems. The signal (data) flow between the subsystems is not shown in Figure 3.

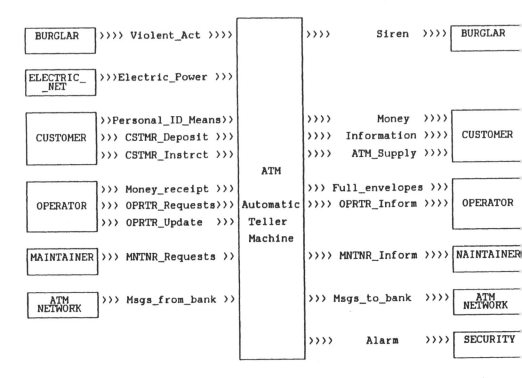

Fig. 2: The ATM in its environment

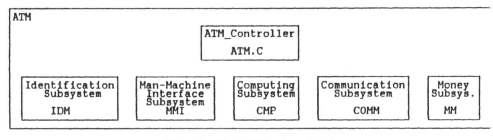

Fig. 3: The ATM subsystems.

Basic Techniques Used in the Analysis Process

The Statechart: As mentioned, major activities of the controller in
the conceptual model are described as a finite state machine. This
behaviour is usually presented graphically by conventional state
transition diagrams. These are normally not structured, difficult to
read and not easily comprehensible by the system's customers. IAI
solved this problem by adopting the statecharts approach, a
structured presentation which replaces the commonly accepted state
transition diagrams. This approach was developed by Harel while
consulting for IAI (HARL87). The statecharts employ the notions of
depth and levels of detail, the ability to split states into
components, thus allowing the specifications of concurrency,
independence and synchronization in various ways and at all levels.

In the following paragraphs we will demonstrate their application,
using the example of the mode transition diagram of the Automatic
Teller Machine-ATM mentioned earlier. In our method and in the
course we refer to super-states as "modes of operation" of the
system (briefly "modes"). The modes are used in a way similar to
that of Heninger (HENI80).

In order to be able to read the statecharts we must point out some
of their basic properties. Statecharts are composed of states
(modes) and transitions between them. Each state (mode) has a name
and so does each transition. States (modes) are organized
hierachically and each state may be further decomposed into several
substates. In this decomposition the substates are related to each
other by the AND or by the OR relation.

States are denoted by boxes. An OR state is denoted by a box which
includes other (disjoint) boxes, representing its substates. For
example in Figure 4, the ATM being in the parent state (mode)
Operating-States means that the system is in one of the following
sub-states (sub-modes): Initialization, Customer - Handling,
Maintenance or Closing.

An AND state (mode) is denoted by a box divided into components that
are delineated by dashed lines. When the ATM system is in Operating-
States it is actually also in Communication-States.

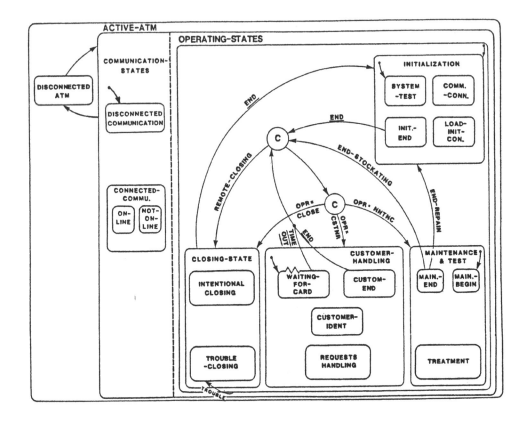

Fig, 4 - The ATM STATECHART

The internal transitions between the submodes are not shown. These will normally be shown in the second level of detail, e.g. the statechart of the Customer-Handling submode. The detailad semantics of the statecharts are presentented in Harel's paper (HARE87).

The conditions affecting the transitions are normally very complex (HENI80). They are functions of external signals and data. It is very important later, in the analysis of the systems, to assure that all conditions and transitions are uniquely defined and that they do not lead to system deadlocks and other undesired phenomena.

Functional and Data Flow Descriptions: The description of the functional behaviour of the system and the signal (data) flow between its modules and their internal activities requires the analysis of the system from both its static and its dynamic aspects. This leads to two distinct types of descriptions. Furthermore, since the analysis methods relate to single computer software systems as well as to multicomputer systems, it is necessary to consider not only data flow between modules and activities but also physical signals connecting subsystems. Disregarding this phenomenon might lead to partially inconsistent presentations of the signal (data) flow in the system. Therefore, throughout this paper we do not refer to data flow but to signal (data) flow.

The static description relates to the decomposition of the system into its subsystems (modules) and the controller, to the steady state description of the activities performed in each one of them and to the signal (data) flow between them. These are analyzed using hierarchical approaches adopted from SADT (ROSS85), some of the concepts and rules used in HOS (HAMI83), and many of the ideas suggested by Parnas (PARN76, PARN79, BRIT81). In the static analysis of the system one has to consider instances where the configuration is being changed during regular operating conditions without changing any physical connections within the system. This is done using technologies such as the MUXBUS (MS1553) or the Ethernet. Each one of these configurations has to be analyzed separately.

Currently we use two graphic approaches to present the static signal (data) flow between the system modules; the N-square chart (LANO79) and a SADT type drawing which have been modified to include the system controller. We also allow the definition of channels between system modules containing many signals or data items.

The dynamic description of the functional behaviour of the system relates to the sequence of operation of the activities within the system modules and their timing. It includes also the description of the dynamic transitions between modes and the dynamic behaviour of the activities or modules, e.g. the time it takes to carry out a calculation or the response time of analog components.

The sequence of the activities and their timing depends on the mode (state) of the system, external and internal events and the current system conditions. The activities can be periodic or demand functions. They can be active throughout a mode (state) or activated only part time within a mode (state). Therefore one has to define, in some later phase of the analysis, the events and conditions which activate the activities, and the modes in which they can be activated. Further one has to specify the events and conditions occurring as a result of the operation of the activities and the dynamic transfer functions of the activities.

The analysis of dynamic processes describing the sequences of activities in the system and their timing requires a graphic presentation of the many possible continuously changing threads of activities within the system. This is done using Statecharts which "fold" together all the different threads of activities which can occur in a given process in response to random sequences of external and internal triggering events. Each one of the processes are thus defined by a couple of diagrams; a DFD type diagram (GANE79) describing the data flow between the activities and a statechart describing the order in which the process activities are performed.

The Evolving Specification Documents: According to the conventional waterfall life cycle and various software development standards, engineers are required to prepare elaborate systems requirements specification documents for the systems software requirements review (SRR). These types of documents are voluminus, difficult to read and can normally not be analyzed thorougly. They can be prepared only after very extensive work taking long periods of time. We therefore recommend the preparation of short intermediate documents which are enhanced during the analysis phases. These intermediate partial specifications should be analyzed as early as possible by all concerned, including the customers. They should be written in such a way that it will be possible later to simply bind them together as the complete final system specification. This approach is similar to the one suggested in the SADT method, where each level of the functional decomposition is analyzed thoroughly by all concerned with the project (readers and commentors) and is agreed upon before proceeding with the analysis of the lower functional levels.

In order to adopt the concept of evolving specification documents we have to reshape the structure of requirements documents as they are described, for example, by DOD Standard 2167(DO2167). This concept has been tried at IAI in various projects. It has been justified by the many misunderstandings that have been discovered during early phases of analysis before proceeding with system development based on wrong assumptions. We have developed a preliminary new structure for the specification documents to match this approach.

Computerized Tools: The systems specifications developed using the IAI method of analysis are very complex. They have to be documented and analyzed using computerized tools. Unfortunately, in the past, none of the availalble tools supported the documentation and analysis of the system as suggested by the IAI method. Therefore, IAI supported the development of a new computerized tool, STATEMATE, build by AD-CAD (ILOG87). This tool supports the system analysis process. Using it, one can document functional and non-functional descriptions and requirements. The functional descriptions and requirements are those which can be tested and analyzed. The non-functional ones are entered as free text. The text is entered for every object defined in the system, using an advanced word processor with graphic capabilities (GLYP85). The functional descriptions and requirements are entered into the system using three graphic editors; a statechart editor, a module editor and an activity editor. Other information is entered by filling out different forms for various kinds of objects.

Consistency checks and logic analysis of the static behaviour is being performed on all the data generated throughout the iterative system analysis process. This analysis requires the definition of a formal language for the description of systems objects e.g. events, conditions, activities, actions and variables (signals). Special semantics were defined by AD-CAD using algebraic and logical expressions. The use of the formal language allows the computerized analysis of the information. The tool also allows the simulation of the system's dynamic behaviour.

THE ANALYSIS PROCESS

Following the description of the basic principles, the conceptual model, some of and the techniques and tools, we will proceed with the discussion of the suggested system analysis process taught in the course. It is assumed that very little is known about the system in the early phases of the analysis. Therefore, the analysis process has to be an iterative one. The analysis of the system, its design and description are stepwise refined. In each level of the decomposition one has to consider all possible views of the system, the logic modules view, the operating modes view, the process (activity) view and the physical view. In this analysis the logic module view relates to the logic subsystems/modules and their signal and data flow. The operating modes view relates to the modes of the system and the transitions between them. The process view describes the static and dynamic behaviour of the processes performed during each mode. The physical view describes the mapping of the logic subsystems to the real hardware.

Basic systems analysis steps are described in the following paragraphs. All of them are applied iteratively at each level, level after level, as many times as it is required in order to completely specify the system and its design. Most of the steps are followed and taught in the course except for the more advanced ones relating to the controller design and discussions of system and hardware architectures.

a. Statement of Need (SON) and Scope. The first step in the development process is the analysis of the need and the basic scope of the system. The scope of the system should include a general description of the main functions to be carried out by the system. This phase is normally performed by the customer and results in a rough description of the system with some guidelines as to the nature of its development, e.g. its development as a family of products (systems, software), consideration of future changes, modes of operation and technologies to be used in the project.

b. The Definition of the System in its Environment. The initial step carried out by the systems analyst is the definition of the system in its environment. First, the boundaries of the system under development have to be defined. Their definition is not trivial and can be a very complex and time consuming activity. Afterwards one should proceed with the listing of all the environmental systems which are connected to the system under development. For example, typical environmental systems of the Automatic Teller Machine-ATM are shown in Figure 2.

Once the environmental systems are defined, the engineer has to specify the main (top level) signals (data) flowing between these systems and the system under development. At this stage the engineer has to describe briefly, in two or three sentences, each environmental system and all of its identified signals and data.

c. The Definition of the Systems Modes. At this phase it is necessary to define with the customer the basic operating modes of the system using the statecharts. In the initial analysis one has to consider basic modes such as; Initilization, Test, Customer-Handling and Closing. The submodes of the operating modes should also be specified and described in this stage. A typical example of the upper level modes of the ATM are shown in Figure 4. (The figure includes also possible top level transitions).

d. Top Level Modular Decomposition. Knowing the scope of the system as it is defined in the SON and the basic operating modes it is possible to perform an initial modular decomposition and to identify the main (top level) system hardware and software subsystems or logic modules. This early identification of the subsystems and the modules might seem strange to software analysts using Data Flow Diagrams (DFDs). They first develop detailed DFDs and only later, following their analysis, they suggest the modular structure of the system. The latter approach leads to special unique decompositions for every project and to the resulting development of new original software modules. Such an approach is not common in any field of engineering, where following a brief limited systems analysis the engineers suggest a conceptual system design as a basis for further economic analysis, more detailed system analysis and design. Adopting this approach one can develop the system, reusing previous typical specifications and design templates of known subsystems rather than redeveloping them for each project. We stress here the reuse of typical specifictions and their adaptation to each particular project. We do not believe that, in most cases, it is possible to reuse major complex designs of subsystems since they have to be adapted to the particular needs of a project. But, the reuse of existing typical specifications and typical design templates, as a basis for the development of the new systems, can considerably increase the productivity of system development (LAVI84, LOES85). Such approaches are common in most fields of engineering.

In the structural decomposition process and in the determination of the main subsystems and modules one should consider such basic concepts as the design for change (where all future changes that are related to one another should be, if possible, localized within one module) and the concept of abstract interfaces (which allows later substitiution of entire subsystems by new ones). These rules apply to all levels of the hierarchical decomposition of the system.

Major criteria used in the decomposition process are outlined in a previous paper (LAVI84). One major criterion should also be emphasized here. The decomposition should consider the possibility that each subsystem or moudle can be developed by a separate (internal or external) subcontractor.

e. <u>System Performance Analysis and Partial SRR</u>. The preparation of a partial system specification and the conducting of a partial SRR, as suggested in the section on the evolving specification documents, are due at this stage.

f. <u>The System Architecture Design</u>. The system architectures should be considered at this stage or earlier. For example the architectures of multicomputer systems, the communication system and the data collection system.

g. <u>Identification of Activities and Detailed Signal (data) Flow</u>. The activities performed in each subsystem (module) and the detailed signal flows are now determined. The approach suggested is to identify the major system outputs and the necessary inputs to all subsystems. Once the data (signal) flows are identified, one proceeds with the identification of all the activities within the subsystems necessary for the generation of the internal and external outputs.

h. <u>Logic and Dynamic Analysis and Controller Design</u>. The detailed behavioural analysis of the system and the preliminary design of the conceptual controller are performed at this phase. This activity is divided into three parts: detailed analysis of the major operating modes of the system and the transitions between them, analysis of the processes being performed by the system in each one of the modes and the design of the controller.

<u>Operating modes and transitions between them</u>. The operational modes and the transitions between them, which were defined during the previous phases, are analyzed in depth. This is done using the Statecharts and their semantics.

<u>Analysis of the Processes</u>. The processes performed by the system during the different operating modes are analyzed in this stage. The analysis takes into account the activities in the sub-systems previously defined and the signal flows between them. These processes are defined as responses to random series of external or internal events.

As mentioned earlier, each process is defined by two complementary diagrams:

1. An activity chart - a DFD which also includes a control function and control signals.

2. A Statechart describing the order and timing of the activities in each process,

<u>The Controller Design</u>. Once system's modes and processes are defined, it is possible to suggest an initial design for the system conceptual controller. This controller has to determine, for example, the transitions between the modes and the activations of the system processes, the sequencing of activities within a process and the changes in the system configuration.

It is important to point out that the operating scenarios of the system and its resulting logic design might change many times during its life cycle. This should be accounted for during this phase of the analysis and the design of the controller.

i. <u>Consistency Checks, Rapid Prototyping and System Simulation</u>. Consistency checks and logic analysis of the static behaviour of the system should be performed on all the data generated throughout the iterative system analysis process. These analyses are performed when desired by the analyst. Static analysis alone is not sufficient. The dynamic complexity of these systems is so large that its evaluation requires good computerized simulations. These simulations can be started only after enough dynamic information has been derived and entered during the previous two steps. Currently the STATEMATE tool allows various kinds of simulations; step by step or batch, deterministic or random.

Using typical specifications of known subsystems and their simulation models, previously constructed during the development of similar systems by the manufacturer, it is possible to simulate the behaviour of new systems in the early analysis phases. This requires a database of the models of typical subsystems and the development of the control algorithm for the particular new system. These simulations can be used as operational rapid prototypes of the new system and can be evaluated by the customers.

COURSE OBJECTIVES, STRUCTURE & CONTENTS

Course objectives. It is expected that at the end of the course participants will be able to:

a. Read a requirements specification document of an ECS which includes both hardware and software or only software and analyze its contents.

b. Analyze an "unfamiliar" system or sub-system, define its requirements with a "client" in a systematic way and prepare a requirements specification document. The definition and analysis of the system will include:

- Definition of the system in its environment.

- Identification of sub-systems and their definition.

- Analysis of process signal (data) flow between the system and its environment and between its sub-systems.

- Definition of the main operating modes of the system.

- Analysis of transitions between the modes (top levels) and determination of the control signals required.

- Basic analysis of the static and dynamic processes of the system.

c. Analyze possible future changes of the system and their influence on the specification and development of the system.

d. Be familiar with STATEMATE, its capabilities and operation.

Teaching Method: Lecture time in the course is limited to **30%** of the time available. Major emphasis is placed on the solution of exercises and **70%** of the time is devoted to their discussion in class. For this purpose we developed a class project which is the basis for all the course exercises. The project is the analysis of the Automatic Teller Machine (ATM). The advantage of this project is that all the students are familiar with these machines and we can concentrate our exercises and discussions on the basic analysis problems and issues rather than on the explanation of a system which is entierly unknown to the students.

Course Content

The structure of the course is described in Table 1. In the following paragraphs we describe each chapter and the corresponding exercises.

Chapter 1 - Introduction: In this chapter we discuss the analysis of modern multi-level multi-computer systems. This is followed by an overall survey of the IAI analysis method and its economic advantages.

Chapter 2 - Iterative Analysis Fundamentals and the ECS Model: In this chapter we introduce the conventional systems development life cycle, discuss its limitations and present our alternative lifecycle. This is followed by a thorough discussion of the ECS model and a deeper overall presentation of the IAI analysis approach and the concept of evolving documents. The last part is devoted to the features of good requirements specifications.

Chapter 3 - Top Level Specifications: The preparation of the top level system specifications for the initial discussions with the customer are discussed. A major issue in this chapter is the determination of the system's boundaries and the identification of the environmental systems and their inferfaces with the system. In the exercise we present to the students the ATM SON and a top level specification. The students are required to analyze the specification and to comment on its quality based on a list of questions.

Chapter 4 - Functional Decomposition: The principles of functional decomposition and their adaptation to decomposition into logic modules are discussed. In the lecture we introduce also basic principles supporting functional decomposition such as abstraction, information hiding and coupling. This is followed by practical considerations that should be made during the decomposition, such as relations between the requirements specification and the top level design.

In the exercise the students are · given three ATM decompositions. They are requested to analyze them and to suggest an alternative solution. Following the discussion of the student's solution a "school-book solution" is suggested and discussed.

Chapter 5 - Analysis of Changes and Systems Families: Parnas's concepts of software change analysis generalized to ECS system problems are presented in this chapter. The lecture covers methods used in the preparation of lists of future changes and criteria for their evaluations. This is followed by a discussion of the development of systems product families based on Parnas's paper on program families.

In the exercise we conduct a brain storming session during which the students are requested to suggest future changes to the ATM system. These are later analyzed and prioritized according to their chances of being materialized and implemented. The students are also expected to identify which subsystems are affected by the suggested changes. From this they are asked to evaluate once more the modular decomposition of the ATM.

Chapter 6 - Operational Mode Analysis and Statecharts: The concepts of modes are discussed. This is followed by a discussion of state transition diagrams currently used and their limitation. Then we introduce the Statecharts techniques.

In the exercise the students are expected to analyze Statecharts describing the top level modes of the ATM system and their transitions.

Chapter 7 - Data Flow and Static Acivities: In this chapter we first discuss the importance of inter-modular data flow analysis. It is followed by the presentation of methods which assist in the determination of the data flow. The methods discussed are based on SADT techniques such as the identification of major outputs and the data needed for their generation by all the modules of the system. At the end of the lecture we discuss techniques for the identification of the activities in each module needed for the generation of those outputs.

In the exercise the students are expected to determine the data flows between the previously defined ATM subsystems. Then they are requested to identify the activities in each subsystem needed for the generation of these data flows. The example used in the exercise is the determination of the data flow and activities for the Money Withdrawal output.

Table 1 - Course Structure

chapter No	Chapter Title	Associated Exercise
1	Introduction	
2	Iterative Analysis Fundamentals, the ECS Model	
3	Top Level Specifications	Analysis of ATM Top Level Specification
4	Functional Decomposition	ATM Decomposition into Sub-systems
5	Analysis of Changes and System Families	Analysis of Changes of the ATM
6	Operational Modes Analysis & Statecharts	ATM Operational Mode Analysis
7	Data flow & Static Activities Analysis	1. Analysis of Activities and Data flow of the ATM 2. Concluding Exercise 1 - Decomposition of one of the ATM's subsystems and analysis of its data-flow
8	Mode Transition Analysis	Decomposition of the ATM Customer Handling Mode into submodes
9	Dynamic Process Analysis	1. Analysis of Basic ATM Processes 2. Concluding exercises 2 - Complete analysis of a computer controlled washing machine
10	Requirements Specification Documents, their Preparation and Checking.	

Chapter 8 - Mode Transition Analysis: Methods for the identification of events and conditions governing the transitions are discussed in this chapter. We also present related topics such as the timing of transitions and mode change processes.

In the exercise the students are expected to decompose the "Customer Handling" mode of the ATM into it's submodes and to identify the events, the conditions and the signals (or data) which implement or affect those conditions and events.

Chapter 9 - Dynamic Process Analysis: The techniques described above for the presentation of dynamic processes, e.g. the use of activity chart and state chart pairs, are presented and demonstrated using an example.

In the exercise the students are expected to analyze the ATM money-deposit-process using those techniques.

Chapter 10 - Requirements Specification Documents; The last chapter is devoted to a review of the analysis process, to the preparation of final specification documents and to analysis and simulation methods used in their evaluation. We include in the lecture a suggested structure for such a document, covering all systems aspects presented in the course. This is necessary since current specification standards do not cover many of the aspects studied in the course which are necessary in a good specification document.

Concluding Exercises: The students are given two concluding exercises. In the first they are expected to decompose one of the ATM subsystems, to determine its internal signal (data) flows and activities and to prepare a basic specification based on it.

In the second exercise the students are expected to analyze and prepare a complete specification of a computer controlled automatic washing machine for which a basic SON is given.

Course Scheduling

The course is being taught in various styles; extended courses and short courses. The first courses were taught as part of IAI ECS software engineering retraining programs. In this framework the course was distributed over periods of several months(LAVI87). This allowed us to give more homework, to have more extensive discussions of the exercises and to give a final project. About 100 hours were devoted to this course. This framework also allowed us to cover more subjects such as handling of undesired events (PAWV76) and abstract interfaces and to teach a tool in the course.

We could not afford to spend that much time during engineering enhancement courses. We could devote to these courses at most five days. This required the deletion of some subjects mentioned above, the final project and the hands-on laboratory using tools to document the specifications. Another disadvantage is the fact that you cannot expect students to do much homework and we had to run all of the exercises in class, analyze the student's solutions between classes and to prepare the class discussion based on actual student's work. This can be done successfully with very careful scheduling of the course. Recently we have decided to give the course on a one day per week basis for six weeks. This works out very well. It allows us to give two concluding exercises during the course and more homework and also to spend more time in class discussions.

Course Laboratory

During the first course all the documentation of the specifications developed during the exercise was done manually because the existing PSL/PSA system was not very user-friendly. For some of the following courses we built a special tool based on ORACLE, a relational data base. This had a tremendous impact, as it allowed the students to document their final projects using the tool. Currently in the short courses we only introduce and demonstrate STATEMATE, the tool we are using in the analysis. There are two reasons for this: lack of time during the short course (it takes one to two days to teach the tool) and the current lack of enough workstations in the educational laboratory. This fact does not cause too many difficulties as all the participants have workstations in their plants. We provide them with the necessary manuals and consulting services as soon as they start to work with the tool on their projects.

Course Materials

The course materials include a book containing about 300 vugraphs, a set of reprints of papers, a set of exercises, and a sample specification of a small system.

STUDENTS AND INSTRUCTORS

The student population in the courses varies widely. In both the retraining courses and in the enhancement courses we have had students with lots of engineering experience as well as students with practically no experience. Undoubtedly the experienced students are more active in the course discussions. They relate the problems, as they are presented in the exercises, to their real project work.

We would like to make one iteresting observation regarding the students. Students who are not good during our course seem to turn out to be poor analysits in practice. That means that good analysts have to have special congenital traits and must be able to look at problems from an overall systems view, disregrarding unnecessary details in early phases of the analysis.

Both instructors who taught most of the courses and who led the class exercises discussions have a Ph.D in computer systems and control engineering and extensive experience in the analysis and development of complex systems. This is very important if one wants to stimulate good discussions in the class and tries to reveal real practical problems in the analysis. Even though we took the ATM as a relatively simple example it is possible, with enough experience, to project from its analysis to problems which are associated with the development of large and complex systems.

LESSONS LEARNED

The course is an evolutionary one. We have been working closely with our graduates on their projects. Based on the problems we have met, we have enhanced our method and incorporated new research results and experiences into our courses. Fortunately, we did not have to change our basic approaches throughout the years. We only had to augment and refine the approach and the course. Based on our experience we can summarize some of the lessons we have learned:

1. Systems analysis is not a secret, it can be taught!

2. Training engineers to pursue a coherent analysis approach can save industry endless hours in system development and unnecessary development cycles.

3. Engineers have to have the natural traits for the analysis of large and complex systems. Having these traits alone without learning the systematic use of analysis methods is not sufficient. Training is a must!

4. The course is effectve also for students who are not born systems engineers. It teaches them a systematic analysis method and it can guide them in their work to get adequate results.

5. The subject is not widely known and one has to exert tremendous effort to sell the approach, as most senior managers are not familiar with methodologies of systems engineering. Therefore in addition to the courses we have set up short seminars, half to one day long, to teach managers the basic principles and convince them that they can ask for better systems analysis and specifications from their engineers and get it.

6. Six day workshops are not sufficient. These have to be followed up by advanced workshops. The subject is very complex to study and to master. Participation in our basic course is just an opening break and following it, people have to gain experience in the field. To achieve this, graduates need still expert advise and consulting. This we are doing by actually consulting with our graduates continuously on many projects. This experince is similar to the one described by Pietrasanta (PIE286).

7. The course instructors must spend at least half of their time consulting on advanced projects and do independent research on new major problems which appear daily. If this is neglected the course material will soon become obsolete.

8. Teaching an extensive course without the availability of an automated tool, such as STATEMATE, supporting the analysis, is not effective. It is impossible to do the multiview analysis without a computerized data base and analysis tool.

Future Developments

As mentioned, we are continuously working with our graduates on their projects. This helps to define our current research which at present addresses the following subjects.

1. Advanced methods for the analysis of multilevel RT/DFD and methods for the identification of the events stimulating the processes.

2. Methods for the analysis and presentation of multilevel systems in which some of the subsystems have many occurrences, such as the case of a command and control system controlling several identical "objects" performing simultaneously different missions.

3. The architecture of the system controller whose dynamic behaviour is a function of the mode changes and the dynamics of the system's processes. We feel that better understanding of the controller's structure can improve the analysis.

4. Analysis of the levels of interfacing necessary for the complete requirement specification of the systems. We start with the logic interfaces, determined in the SADT like analysis and continue to the actual physical interfaces described by the physical view. We expect a multi-level model (probably with 3-5 levels) resembling somehow the ISO model. .

We are currently planning the following courses:

1. A short course for managers of probably five to eight hours duration.

2. A short course on the operation of using STATEMATE.

3. An advenced course, 4-5 days duration, which stresses the following subjects; RT-DFD process analysis, the semantics of STATEMATE, advanced considerations in systems decomposition into their logic modules or subsystems, abstract interfaces and their relation to the logic and physical view, handling of unexpected events, performance analysis and specifications, statistical dynamic testing (simulation) of the specifications and more discussions about the structure of the evolving and final specification documents.

Acknowledgements

The authors would like to thank all the engineers in IAI who contributed through their questions, suggestions and discussions to the development of the method and the course. Specially we would like to thank Eran Kessler and Ronie Rokach who developed and taught the course laboratories.

REFERENCES

BALZ82   Balzar, R, Swartout, W., "On the Inevitable Interwining of Specification and Implementation", Communication of the ACM, Vol 25, Mo 7, July 1982 pp. 438-440.

BRIT81   Britton-Heninger, K., Parker A. R., Parnas, D. L., "A Procedure for Designing Abstract Interfaces for Device Modules", Proceeding of the Fifth International Conference on Software Engineering, March 1981, pp. 195-205.

DO2167   DOD Standard 2167, "Defense Systems Software Development", Department of Defense, Wanshinton DC, June 1985.

GLYP85   (-), "Glyph Word Processing System", John Bryce (Glasgow) Ltd., Talpiot, Jerusalem, Israel, May 1985.

GANE79   Gane, C., Sarson, T., "Structured Systems Analysis: Tools and Techniques", Prentice Hall 1979.

HAMI83   Hamilton, M., Zeldin, S., "The Functional Life Cycle Model and Its Automation: USE. IT", The Journal of Systems and Software, Vol 3, No. 1, pp. 25-62, March 1983.

HARE87   Harel, D., "Statecharts: A Visual Formalism for Complex System", in Science of Computer Programming, Vol 8, pp. 231-274, Nort-Holland, 1987.

HENI80   Heninger, K.L., "Specifying Software Requirements for Complex Systems: New Techniques and their Applications". IEEE Transactions on Software Engineering, January 1980, pp. 2-13.

ILOG87   (-), "Statemate - The Visual Appreach", i-Logix Inc. 22 Third Avenue, Burlington, Ma 01803, 1987.

LAVI84   Lavi, J.Z., "A Systems Engineering Approach to Software Engineering", IEEE Proc. Software Process Workshop, Egham, UK, Feb. 1984, pp. 49-57.

LAVI86   Lavi, J.Z., Kessler, E., "An Embedded Computer Systems Analysis Method, "in Procedings of Israel First Conference on Computer Systems and Software Engineering" Tel Aviv, June 1986.

LAVI87   Lavi, J.Z., Ben-Porat, M., Ben-David, A., "IAI Corporate
          Software Engineering Training and Education Program" IEEE
          Transactions on Software Engineering, November 1987.

LANO79   Lano, R. J., "A Technique for Software and Systems Design",
          TRW Series on Software Engineering, North Holland
          Publishing Company, Amsterdam, 1979.

LOES85   Loesh, R. E., "Improving Productivity Through Standard
          Design Templates", Data Processing, Butterworth & Co., Vol
          27, No. 9 November 1985, pp. 57-59.

MCFA82   McFadyen, W. S., "A Cohesive Methodology for the
          Development of Large Real-Time Systems", Journal of
          Telecommunication Networks, Vol. No. 3, Feb. 1982, pp.
          265-280.

MS1553   MIL-STD-1553B, "U.S.A Military Standart, Aircraft Internal
          Time Devision Command Response Multiplex Data Bus", 1976.

PARN76   Parnas, D. L., "On the Design & Development of Program
          Families", IEEE Transactions on Software Engineering, Vol.
          SE-2, No. 1, pp. 1-9,1976.

PARN79   Parnas, D. L., "Designing Software for Ease of Extention &
          Contraction", IEEE Transaction on software Engineering,
          Vol. SE-5, No 2, pp. 128-137, 1979.

PAWU76   Parnas, D. L., Wuerges, H., "Respnse tp Undesired Events in
          Systes Software", Proceedings of Second International
          Conference, on Software Engineering, pp. 427-446, 1976.

PIE186   Pietrasanta, A., Personal discussion during conference on
          Software Engineering Education, Pittsbourgh, 1987

PIE286   Pietrasanta, A.," Keynote Address in "Proceedings of 1987
          Conference on Software Engineering Education". North
          Holland, 1988 .

ROSS85   Ross, D. T., "Applications and Extensions of SADT",
          Computer, Vol 18, No, 4, April 1985, PP. 25-35.

TIEC77   Tiechroew, D., Hershy, E. A. III, "PSL/PSA : A Computer
          Aided Technique for Structured Documentation and Analysis
          of Information Processing Systems", IEEE Transactions on
          Software Engineering, January 1977, pp. 41-48.

WHIT85   White, M. S., Lavi, J, Z., "Embedded Computer System
          Requirements Workshop", Computer, Vol. 19, No. 4, April
          1985

A Course on Software Engineering for Concurrent Systems

Kuo-Chung Tai
Department of Computer Science
Box 8206
North Carolina State University
Raleigh, North Carolina 27695-8206, USA

Abstract. This paper describes a graduate level course that covers concepts, techniques and tools for the specification, design, coding, and validation of concurrent software. This course is intended to transfer practical software engineering technology for the production of reliable concurrent software systems. One unique aspect of this course is the use of a collection of tools developed at NCSU for testing and debugging concurrent software.

1. Introduction

Software engineering has become an indispensable part of computer science education. Many computer science departments are offering software engineering courses, which cover concepts, techniques, and tools for the requirement analysis, specification, design, coding, validation, maintenance, and management of computer software.

With the decreasing price and increasing performance of computer hardware, the use of concurrent (parallel or distributed) systems is growing rapidly. The need for developing concurrent software systems has stimulated active research on software engineering issues such as

* how to specify concurrency?
* how to design the structure of a concurrent program?
* how to design or select concurrent languages for implementing concurrent programs?
* how to validate concurrent programs?

Appendix 1 provides a list of major journals and conference proceedings that publish research results on software engineering for concurrent systems. A recent paper by Shatz and Wang [Sha87] provides an introduction to software engineering topics on the development of distributed systems.

Due to the increasing demand for concurrent software systems and the maturity of software engineering technology for developing such systems, there is a need to offer courses on software engineering for concurrent systems. Such courses are intended to transfer practical software engineering technology for the production of reliable concurrent software systems. Currently, there exists no model or textbook for such courses.

Since 1985 the author has taught at North Carolina State University a graduate level course on software engineering for concurrent systems. The purpose of this paper is to describe this course. The paper is organized as follows. Section 2 provides a brief review of major topics on software engineering for concurrent systems. Section 3 describes the content of the course. Section 4 describes a set of concurrent programming tools developed at NCSU for this course. Section 5 concludes the paper.

2. Software Engineering Topics on the Development of Concurrent Software Systems

The life cycle of concurrent software is not different from that of sequential software. But the development of concurrent software involves problems that do not exist in the development of sequential software. Below is a brief review of major software engineering topics on the development of concurrent software.

Specification of Concurrency: A number of formal models and languages for specifying concurrency have been developed. Since different models and languages consider different aspects of concurrency and have different limitations, it is difficult to make a comparison between them. Formal specification of concurrency provides several advantages. First, a formal specification is unambiguous and prevents misunderstandings. Second, a formal specification can be analyzed for error detection. Third, a formal specification can help the validation of an implementation of the specification. For a complicated concurrent system, it is often difficult or impossible to derive a formal, complete specification of the system. Still, an attempt to derive as much formal specification as possible for a concurrent system will greatly improve the quality of the system.

Partitioning and Allocation of a Concurrent Program: In the design stage of a concurrent program, it is necessary to partition the program into processes and allocate these processes to processors. The partitioning and allocation of a concurrent program are subject to cost, configuration, performance, reliability, and other constraints.

Concurrent Languages: Quite a few concurrent constructs and languages have been developed and studied [And83,Fil84]; they can be divided into two categories, one based on shared variables and the other based on message passing. (Concurrent languages in the second category are called distributed languages.) Most of the existing concurrent programs were written using a mixture of sequential programming languages, assembly languages, and operating system commands. As a result, such programs have a portability problem and are difficult to understand and maintain. With the availability of high quality compilers for powerful concurrent languages such as Ada, Concurrent C, and Modula-2, the use of high-level concurrent languages to develop concurrent software is becoming a reality.

Validation of Concurrent Software: Like a sequential program, a concurrent program can be validated by using formal verification (i.e. proof of correctness), static analysis, testing, and debugging. However, the validation of concurrent programs is more difficult than that of sequential programs due to the existence of synchronization between concurrent processes. How to detect synchronization errors is the major problem in the validation of concurrent programs.

3. The NCSU Course on Software Engineering for Concurrent Systems

3.1 Course Objective

The objective of this course is to study concepts, techniques and tools for the development of concurrent software systems. This course is open to graduate students who have taken an operating system design course in which the concept of concurrent programming and the semaphore and monitor constructs are covered.

The selection of materials for this three-credit semester course is difficult since many papers have been published on each of the four topics discussed in section 2. Our selection of materials is based on the following considerations:

(a) This course is intended to transfer practical software engineering technology that can be applied to improve the reliability and reduce the development cost of concurrent software.

(b) Students taking this course generally have no experience in writing concurrent programs and have little knowledge of concurrent languages.

(c) Students generally will begin their career with implementing and validating programs. The high-level design and specification of programs are usually done by experienced programmers.

Thus, this course puts major emphasis on the topics of concurrent languages and validation techniques and discusses these two topics before other topics. In the discussion of validation techniques, the emphasis is on analysis, testing and debugging, not formal verification.

3.2 Course Structure

The course is divided into seven parts. Below is a brief summary of these seven parts. Appendix 2 of this paper provides a reading list for the course. This reading list contains materials that either have been used in the course or are likely to be used in the future. Thus, the reading list contains more than enough materials for a semester course.

Part 1: Introduction. This part provides a review of software engineering for both sequential and concurrent software systems.

Part 2: Concurrent Constructs and Languages Based on Shared Variables. This part covers the semaphore, conditional critical region, and monitor constructs and the Concurrent Pascal and Modula-2 languages. Students are required to use UCSD Pascal to write concurrent programs based on the semaphore and monitor constructs. (UCSD Pascal supports the semaphore construct and the declaration of concurrent processes. We have implemented a tool in UCSD Pascal that simulates the monitor construct by using semaphores.)

Part 3: Validation of Concurrent Programs Based on Shared Variables. This part discusses how to test and debug concurrent programs that use semaphores and monitors. Students are required to use a set of tools developed at NCSU to test and debug their concurrent UCSD Pascal programs. (See section 4 for the discussion of concurrent programming tools developed at NCSU.)

Part 4: Concurrent Constructs and Languages Based on Message Passing.
This part covers the send/receive and remote procedure call constructs
and several distributed languages including CSP (Communicating
Sequential Processes), DP (Distributed Processes), Ada, and Concurrent
C. Students are required to solve several concurrent problems using
Ada.

Part 5: Validation of Concurrent Programs Based on Message Passing.
This part addresses how to analyze, test, and debug distributed
programs. Students are required to use a set of tools developed at
NCSU to test and debug their concurrent Ada programs.

Part 6: Specification of Concurrency. This part discusses several
models and languages for specifying concurrency.

Part 7: Design of Concurrent Programs. This part covers issues on the
design of a concurrent program, such as partitioning and allocation.

The interleaving of the topics of concurrent languages and validation
techniques in parts 2 through 5 allows students to apply validation
techniques immediately after they have finished writing concurrent
programs.

3.3 Textbooks and Handouts

There exists no single book that covers all of the subjects mentioned
in section 3.2. The book Coordinated Computing: Tools and Techniques
for Distributed Software, written by R. E. Filman and D. P. Friedman,
covers many models and languages for concurrent programming. The book
Ada: Concurrent Programming, written by N. Gehani, provides a detailed
description of the concurrent features of Ada and shows many
concurrent Ada programs. Several books on software validation are
available, but none of them concentrates on the analysis, testing and
debugging of concurrent software.

Appendix 2 of the paper indicates the papers and book chapters that
either have been used in the course or are likely to be used in the
future. Lecture notes are prepared to summarize the content of papers
covered in the course. Copies of lecture notes and reprints of papers
are distributed to students.

3.4 Homework, Programming Assignments, and Term Papers/Projects

Many homework problems have been developed for this course. These problems generally deal with the following issues: the determination of the correctness of concurrent programs, the comparison of various concurrent constructs and languages, and the implementation of one concurrent construct/language using another.

As mentioned earlier, students are required to implement concurrent programs using UCSD Pascal and Ada. The programming problems assigned to students include classical concurrent problems, such as the concurrent readers and writers problem, the dining philosophers problem and the sleeping barber problem. At NCSU, UCSD Pascal compilers are available on SAGE computers and various personal computers, and Verdix Ada compilers are available on MicroVAX and Sequent Balance computers. Also, Concurrent C compilers are available on VAX computers and Sun workstations.

In this course, each student is required to do a term paper or project for an in-depth study of a specific topic on software engineering for concurrent systems. Many of these papers and projects have produced interesting results. In particular, some of these projects have contributed to the concurrent programming tools discussed in the next section.

4. Concurrent Programming Tools Developed at NCSU

It is well known that a monitor can be simulated by using semaphores [Hoa74]. Since UCSD Pascal supports the semaphore construct and the declaration of concurrent processes, the simulation of a monitor in UCSD Pascal is not difficult. We have developed a tool for supporting the monitor construct in UCSD Pascal; this tool is an improved version of the implementation described in [Bod83,84].

We have also developed a set of tools for testing and debugging concurrent programs. Such tools are needed for the following reasons [Tai85,87a]. An execution of a concurrent program P exercises a sequence of synchronization events, called a <u>synchronization sequence</u> or <u>SYN-sequence</u>. (The definition of a SYN-sequence of P depends on the synchronization constructs used in P.) The result of an execution of P is determined by P and the input and SYN-sequence of this execution. Due to the unpredictable progress of concurrent processes in P, multiple executions of P <u>with the same input</u> may exercise different SYN-sequences and may even produce different results.

The nondeterministic execution behavior of concurrent programs creates a problem during the debugging phase. Assume that an execution of a concurrent program P with input X produces an incorrect result and that it is necessary to repeat the SYN-sequence of this erroneous execution in order to collect additional debugging information. However, there is no guarantee that this SYN-sequence will be repeated during one or more nondeterministic executions of P with input X. The problem of how to repeat the SYN-sequence of a previous execution of a concurrent program is referred to as the <u>reproducible testing problem</u> [Tai85]. Let the SYN-sequence exercised during an execution of a concurrent program with a given input be called a <u>feasible SYN-sequence</u> of this program with the given input.

The reproducible testing problem can be solved by forcing a <u>deterministic execution</u> of a feasible SYN-sequence of a concurrent program with a given input. One strategy for solving this problem, called <u>source transformation</u>, is to transform a concurrent program P into another program P' (written in the same language as P) so that any execution of P' with (X,S) as input, where S is a feasible SYN-sequence of P with input X, definitely exercises S and produces the same result as P with input X and SYN-sequence S would. We have applied the source transformation strategy to solve the reproducible testing problem and implement reproducible testing tools for the semaphore, monitor, and send/receive constructs and the Ada and Concurrent C languages [Car86,Pat88,Tai86,87b]. Also, we have implemented tools for collecting the SYN-sequences exercised during executions of concurrent UCSD Pascal program.

The nondeterministic execution behavior of concurrent programs also creates a problem during the testing phase. When testing a concurrent program P with input X, a single execution is insufficient to determine the correctness of P with input X. The reason is that a single execution of P with input X exercises just one of possibly many feasible SYN-sequences of P with input X. In fact, even if P with input X has been executed successfully many times, it is possible that a future execution of P with input X will produce an incorrect result.

To effectively detect errors in P by testing, the following two approaches can be applied. One approach, called <u>multiple execution</u>

testing, is to execute P with each selected input <u>many times</u>. The following methods can be applied to increase the chances of exercising different SYN-sequences during different executions of P with the same input:

(a) Assign different values to the time quantum for round-robin scheduling during different executions of P. This method requires that the time quantum for round-robin scheduling be adjustable by the programmer.

(b) Insert delay statements into P and randomly assign the amount of each delay during different executions of P. This method requires that delay statements for the real-time clock be available.

(c) This method is similar to method (b), but the delay time is based on a virtual-time clock, not the real-time clock. The virtual-time clock can be implemented by creating a process that has lower priority than processes in P and wakes up the processes blocked on delay statements according to the value of the virtual-time clock.

We have developed tools that support the above methods for testing concurrent UCSD Pascal and Ada programs.

The other approach to testing P, called <u>deterministic execution testing</u>, is as follows:

(1) Select a set of tests, each of the form (X,S), where X and S are an input and a SYN-sequence of P respectively.

(2) For each selected test (X,S),
    (2.1) determine whether or not S is feasible for P with input X,
    (2.2) if S is feasible, examine the result produced by P with input X and SYN-sequence S.

The problem in step (2.1), referred to as the <u>SYN-sequence feasibility</u> problem, is slightly different from the reproducible testing problem. A reproducible testing tool, however, can be used to solve the SYN-sequence feasibility problem. The deterministic execution testing approach provides the following advantages:

(a) This approach allows the use of carefully selected SYN-sequences to test a concurrent program.

(b) Assume that an error is detected by an execution of a concurrent program P with input X. After an attempt has been made to fix the error, P can be tested with input X and the SYN-sequence of this erroneous execution in order to make sure that the error has been fixed.

(c) After a concurrent program has been modified for correction or enhancement, the program can be tested with the inputs and SYN-sequences of previous executions of the program in order to make sure that the modification does not introduce new errors. Details of the deterministic execution testing approach and the problems involved in this testing approach are given in [Tai87a].

5. Conclusion

In this paper we have described a course offered at NCSU that covers concepts, techniques and tools for the specification, design, coding, and validation of concurrent software. This course is intended to transfer practical software engineering technology for the production of reliable concurrent software systems. The major emphases of this course are concurrent languages and validation techniques for concurrent software.

Since the use of concurrent systems is growing rapidly, the teaching of concepts, techniques and tools for developing concurrent software systems should become an important subject in computer science education. The course described in the paper is just one example of how to teach software engineering for concurrent systems. Currently a number of computer science departments offer a course on concurrent languages. This language course can be followed by a software engineering course covering the specification, design, and validation of concurrent software. Many computer science departments offer a sequence of two courses on operating systems, with the first course on the principles of operating system design and the second course on the implementation of an operating system project. Some materials on software engineering for concurrent systems can be taught in the second operating system course.

The set of tools developed at NCSU for testing and debugging concurrent software has been demonstrated to be very helpful to students. Currently, students are required to write concurrent programs in UCSD Pascal and Ada. Since the compilers for these two languages run on different machines and under different operating systems, students have to spend a lot of time to learn how to use different operating systems, compilers, and editors. We are in the process of implementing Ada packages to simulate the semaphore and monitor constructs and to support various testing and debugging techniques for these simulated constructs. With these Ada packages, there is no need to use UCSD Pascal to write concurrent programs based on the semaphore and monitor constructs.

Acknowledgment

The author wishes to thank the students who have contributed to the development of the concurrent programming tools described in the paper. Also, the author would like to thank Richard Carver for his comments on this paper.

References

[Age85] Agerberg, J., "The simplest? Ada solution to the dining philosophers problem", ACM Ada Letters, July/August, 1985, 44-48.

[And83] Andrews, G. R., and Schneider, F. B., Concepts and notations for concurrent programming," ACM Computing Surveys, Vol. 15, No.1, March 1983, 3-43.

[Bod83] Boddy, D. E. "Implementing data abstractions and monitors in UCSD Pascal," ACM SIGPLAN Notices, Vol. 18, No. 5, May 1983, 15-24.

[Bod84] Boddy, D. E., "On the design of monitors with priority conditions," ACM SIGPLAN Notices, Vol. 19, No. 2, February, 1984, 38-46.

[Bri73] Brinch Hansen, P., "Testing a multiprogramming system", Software-Practice and Experience, Vol. 3, 1973, 145-150.

[Bri78] Brinch Hansen, P., "Reproducible testing of monitors," Software-Practice and Experience, Vol. 8, 1978, 721-729.

[Cam74] Campbell, R. H., and Habermann, A. N., "The specification of process synchronization by path expressions," Lecture Notes in Computer Science, Vol. 16, Operating Systems, 1974, 87-102.

[Cam79] Campbell, R. H., and Kolstad, R. B., "Path Expressions in Pascal" Proc. 4th Inter. Conf. Software Engineering, 1979, 212-219.

[Car86] Carver, R. H., and Tai, K. C., "Reproducible testing of concurrent programs based on shared variables," Proc. 6th Int. Conf. on Distributed Computing Systems, 1986, 428-433.

[Cla82] Clark, R., and Koehler, S., The UCSD Pascal Handbook, Prentice-Hall, 1982.

[Fai85] Fairley, R. E., Software Engineering Concepts, McGraw-Hill, 1985.

[Fil84] Filman, R. E., and Friedman, D. P., Coordinated Computing: Tools and Techniques for Distributed Software, McGraw-Hill, 1984.

[Gai86] Gait, J, "A probe effect in concurrent programs,"

Software-Practice and Experience, March 1986, 225-233.

[Geh84] Gehani, N., Ada: Concurrent Programming, Prentice-Hall, 1984.

[Geh86] Gehani, N., and Roome, W. D., "Concurrent C," Software-Practice and Experience, Sept. 1986, 821-844.

[Hea85] Headington, M. R., and Oldehoeft, A. E., "Open predicate path expressions and their implementation in highly parallel computing environments," Proc. 1985 Inter. Conf. on Parallel Computing, 1985, 239-246.

[Hel85a] Helmbold, D., and Luckham, D., "Debugging Ada tasking programs," IEEE Software, Vol. 2, No. 2, March 1985, 47-57.

[Hel85b] Helmbold, D., "TSL: task specification language," Proc. Ada Inter. Conf. (ACM Ada LETTERS, Vol. V, Issue 2, Sept./Oct. 1985), 255-274.

[Hoa74] Hoare, C.A.R., "Monitors: an operating system structuring concept," Comm. ACM, Vol. 17, No. 10, Oct. 1974, 549-557.

[Jon87] Jones, S. H., Barkan, R. H., and Wittie, L. D., "Bugnet: a real time distributed debugging system", Proc. 6th Symp. Reliability in Distributed Software and Database Systems, 1987, 56-65.

[LeD85] LeDoux, C. H., and Parker, D. S., "Saving traces for Ada debugging," Proc. Ada Inter. Conf. (ACM Ada LETTERS, Vol. V, Issue 2, Sept./Oct. 1985), 97-108.

[Nie87] Nielsen, K. W., and Shumatre, K., "Designing large real-time systems with Ada", Comm. ACM, Vol. 30, No. 8, August 1987, 695-715.

[Pat88] Patwardhan, M. R., and Tai, K. C., "A debugging environment for Concurrent C", Technical report TR-88-, Dept. of Computer Science, North Carolina State University, 1988.

[Pet85] Peterson, J. A., and Silberschatz, A., Operating system concepts, Addison-Wesley, 1985.

[Ram83] Ramamritham, K., and Keller, R. M., "Specification of synchronizing processes," IEEE Trans. Soft. Eng., Vol. SE-9, No. 6, Nov. 1983, 722-733.

[Rov86] Rovner, P., "Extending Modula-2 to build large, integrate systems", IEEE Software, Vol. 3, No. 6, Nov. 1986, 46-57.

[Sme83] Smedema, C. H., Medema, P., and Boasson, M., The Programming Languages Pascal, Modula, Chill and Ada, Prentice-Hall, 1983.

[Sha86] Shatz, S. M., and Yau, S. S., "A partitioning algorithm for the design of distributed software systems", Information Sciences, April 1986, 165-180.

[Sha87] Shatz, S. M., and Wang, J. P., "Introduction to distributed software engineering", Computer, October 1987, 23-31.

[Tai85]   Tai, K. C., "On testing concurrent programs," Proc. COMPSAC 85, Oct. 1985, 310-317.

[Tai86]   Tai, K. C., and Obaid, E. E., "Reproducible testing of Ada tasking programs" Proc. IEEE 2nd Int. Conf. on Ada Applications and Environments, April 1986, 69-79.

[Tai87a] Tai, K. C., and Carver, R. H., "Testing and Debugging of concurrent software by deterministic execution", Technical report TR-87-19, Dept. of Computer Science, North Carolina State University, 1987.

[Tai87b] Tai, K. C., and Ahuja, S., "Reproducible testing of communication software", Proc. COMPSAC 87, 1987, 331-337.

[Tay83]   Taylor, R.N., "A general-purpose algorithm for analyzing concurrent programs," Comm. ACM, Vol. 26, No. 5, May 1983, 362-375.

[Wel84]   Wellings, A. J., Keeffe, D., and Tomlinson, G. M., "A problem with Ada and resource allocation", ACM Ada Letters, Jan./Feb., 1984, 112-124.

Appendix 1: Major Journals and Conference Proceedings that Publish Papers on Software Engineering for Concurrent Systems

Journals:
* ACM Transaction on Programming Languages and Systems
* Distributed Computing
* IEEE Software
* IEEE Transaction on Software Engineering
* Journal of Parallel and Distributed Computing
* Journal of Systems and Software
* Software - Practice & Experience

Proceedings of the following symposiums and conferences:
* ACM Symposium on Principles of Programming Languages
* ACM Symposium on Principles of Distributed Computing
* ACM Symposium on Principles of Operating Systems
* IEEE Conference on Distributed Computing Systems
* IEEE Conference on Computer Software & Applications
* IEEE Symposium on Real-Time Systems
* International Conference on Software Engineering

Appendix 2: Reading List for Software Engineering on Concurrent
         Systems

Part 1: Introduction
* <u>Software Engineering Concepts</u> by Fairley [Fai85]
* "Introduction to distributed-software engineering" by Shatz
  and Wang [Sha87]

Part 2: Concurrent Constructs and Languages Based on Shared
         Variables
* Sections 1 through 3 of "Concepts and Notations for Concurrent
  Programming" by Andrews and Schneider [And83]
* Chapters 9 and 10 of <u>Operating Systems Concepts</u> by Peterson and
  Silberschatz [Pet85]
* Chapter 9, Concurrency, of <u>The UCSD Pascal Handbook</u> by Clark and
  Koehler [Cla82]
* "Implementing data abstractions and monitors in UCSD Pascal" by
  Boddy [Bod83]
* "On the design of monitors with priority conditions" by Boddy
  [Bod84]
* Section 13.1, Concurrent Pascal, of <u>Coordinated Computing: Tools
  and Techniques for Distributed Software</u> by Filman and Friedman
  [Fil84].
* Chapter 3, Modula, of <u>The Programming Languages Pascal, Modula,
  CHILL, and Ada</u> by Smedema et al. [Sme83]
* "Extending Modula-2 to build large, integrate systems" by Rovner
  [Rov86]

Part 3: Validation of Concurrent Programs Based on Shared Variables
* "Reproducible testing of monitors" by Brinch Hansen [Bri78]
* "Testing a multiprogramming system" by Brinch Hansen [Bri73]
* "A probe effect in concurrent programs" by Gait [Gai86]
* "Testing and Debugging of concurrent software by deterministic
  execution" by Tai and Carver [Tai87a]
* "Reproducible testing of concurrent programs using semaphores,
  conditional critical regions, and monitors" by Carver and Tai
  [Car86]

Part 4: Concurrent Constructs and Languages Based on Message Passing
* Section 4 of [And83].
* Chapter 10, Communicating sequential processes, of [Fil84]
* Section 13.2, Distributed processes, of [Fil84]

* Chapter 14, Ada, of [Fil84]
* Chapters 2 through 6 of <u>Ada: Concurrent Programming</u> by Gehani [Geh84]
* "The simplest? Ada solution to the dining philosophers problem" by Agerberg [Age85]
* "A problem with Ada and resource allocation" by Wellings et al. [Wel84]
* "Concurrent C" by Gehani and Roome [Geh86]

Part 5: Validation of Concurrent Programs Based on Message Passing
* "A general-purpose algorithm for analyzing concurrent programs" by Taylor [Tay83]
* "Reproducible testing of Ada tasking programs" by Tai and Obaid [Tai86]
* "Debugging Ada tasking programs" by Helmbold and Luckham [Hel85a]
* "Saving traces for Ada debugging" by LeDoux and Parker [LeD85]
* "Bugnet: a real-time distributed debugging system" by Jones, Barkan, and Wittie [Jon87]

Part 6: Specification of Concurrency
* "The specification of process synchronization by path expressions" by Campbell and Habermann [Cam74]
* "Path Expressions in Pascal" by Campbell and Kolstad [Cam79]
* "Open predicate path expressions and their implementation in highly parallel computing environments," by Headington and Oldehoeft [Hea85]
* Section 9.1, Petri Nets, of [Fil84]
* "TSL: task sequencing language" by Helmbold [Hel85b]
* "Specification of synchronizing processes" by Ramamritham and and Keller [Ram83]

Part 7: Design of Concurrent Programs
* "Designing large real-time systems with Ada" by Nielsen and Shumatre [Nie87]
* "A partitioning algorithm for the design of distributed software systems" by Shatz and Yau [Sha86]

SEI Demonstration:
Advanced Learning Technologies Project

Scott Stevens
Software Engineering Institute
Carnegie Mellon University

ABSTRACT

The Advanced Learning Technologies Project at the Software Engineering Institute is developing an interactive course on code inspections for software practitioners and students. The course incorporates traditional computer-based instruction with artificial intelligence, interactive video, and digital audio to create a simulation of a group code review process. Through this simulation the student learns about code inspections.

One major goal of this project is to demonstrate the potential use of these technologies in the field of software engineering education. A prototype has been developed to illustrate an approach to the delivery of interactive instruction on code inspections.

UNDERGRADUATE SOFTWARE ENGINEERING EDUCATION

William E. Richardson
United States Air Force Academy

Abstract. Software engineering education is a difficult venture at very best but the difficulty of teaching software engineering ideas at the undergraduate level is even more problematic. The most significant problem in undergraduate software engineering education is, not surprisingly, lack of maturity. From our experience over the last six years this immaturity manifests itself in three different areas: computer science, academics in general, and social and personal relations. Each of the these manifestations of the undergraduate's lack of development has a significant impact on their ability to understand software engineering concepts. The results of our study on the unique pitfalls of undergraduate software engineering education are detailed in the first of the two papers that follow.

We feel that software engineering should be an equal partner in our undergraduate computer science major with the more traditional hardware and software topics. Based on our experiences, we have developed an approach for teaching software engineering which considers the immaturity of undergraduates and attempts to avoid the problems it imposes. The second paper briefly outlines our approach, which is based upon the sound educational principle of iteration of basic concepts and the eventual synthesis of those concepts into second and third level relationships.

ON THE PROBLEMS IN UNDERGRADUATE SOFTWARE ENGINEERING EDUCATION

Introduction

Software engineering education is a difficult venture at very best but the difficulty of software engineering education at the undergraduate level is intensified by several additional and sometimes overriding concerns. The well documented difficulty of designing graduate level software engineering programs is based on such factors as the diversity of the discipline, the immaturity of the tools and techniques, the lack of guiding principles, the variety of the application fields, the magnitude of the problems discussed, and the requirement for design. [RICH86; FREE86] Certainly these same problems are relevant when the software engineering discipline is being introduced in an undergraduate framework. However, these problems are magnified at the undergraduate level by the inexperience of the student, resulting in other difficulties that graduate programs generally choose to ignore.

We began this study of problems in undergraduate software engineering education because we were unhappy with the lack of software engineering understanding our computer science majors had at graduation. It appears that we are not the only ones who are unhappy. Gary Ford recently noted: "Many employers now comment that newly hired computer science graduates are not ready for immediate assignment to software development projects because of their inexperience with large projects, their lack of group programming skills, and a lack of understanding of management and business economics." [FORD86:437] While he states this is not an indictment of computer science curricula, we tend to think that it should be--at least until the time comes that a software engineering undergraduate program is appropriate. However, before we could effectively introduce the concepts of software engineering into our curriculum we needed better insight into the unique problems that plagued our efforts in the early years.

Like most undergraduate computer science programs, we began by introducing software engineering concepts at a very low level--we should call them "implementation" rather than "engineering" concepts. These included, of course, such things as procedural abstraction, information hiding, top down design, modularity, and structured programming. While this "micro" view is still very important, in our opinion it is no longer adequate to fully prepare undergraduate computer scientists--computer science majors today also need an orientation in "macro" and "system" level concepts. [RICH86:99] Therefore, in this paper we use the term "software engineering" to mean a lifecycle, methodological approach to large system development as opposed to the lower level micro view referred to as software engineering in many undergraduate computer science programs.

The Problems

It is absolutely no surprise that the major problem in teaching software engineering to undergraduates is lack of maturity on the part of the student. However, the manifestations of that immaturity are often very surprising. We have divided this immaturity into three different categories for ease of discussion and observation: computer science, academic, and social/personal. The following describes manifestations of these categories of immaturity in our efforts to introduce software engineering concepts into the undergraduate computer science program.

Computer Science Maturity.

Many of the students entering the first course in a computer science major have some preconception of the likely content of the major. Often, that preconception is based on previous computer experience with high school programming courses and computer games of one form or another. More often than not, the notion these students have is that computer science is synonymous with programming. Many of the undergraduate curricula we have seen reinforce that notion by starting those same students in a freshman programming course. It is no wonder, then, that many students enter the computer science major expecting to write code and have no understanding of the discipline of computer science.

Based on this myopic view of the nature of computer science, we have found students often recoil when they are initially forced to study a topic that they cannot "hack" (in the worst possible sense!) their way through. Sometimes this revulsion is based on the lack of "orderliness" they see in programming problems and sometimes, perhaps even most times, the revulsion is because coding is a challenge and fun, while more esoteric topics seem dull by comparison.

Of course, any beginning student is assumed unknowledgeable of even the basics of the discipline or he would not be a beginning student. This immaturity in the theory of computer science makes it very difficult to intelligibly present the second and third level concepts and relationships which abound in software engineering. As Bob Glass stated: "A knowledge of computer science theory is a necessary but not sufficient part of the software engineer's tool bag. Computer science theory sometimes does not work in practice. The software engineer must know enough about the theory to know how to avoid these failures." [GLAS86:77] Consequently, it is difficult to present software engineering, even (or perhaps especially) in abstract, condensed form so that it makes sense to the new computer science student.

The undergraduate student has little or no appreciation for the problem that software engineering is designed to mollify. They have never seen huge software projects which were developed well over budget, are several years late, and still do not satisfying the requirements. We at the Air Force Academy have a leg up in this department since we can easily go to the literature and point to the massive amounts (projected to be $30 billion in 1990 [CANA86]) spent by the DoD each year for the development and maintenance of software.   Unfortunately, because of the students' very limited experience, these figures still provide little motivation to the topic of software engineering.

The computer programming problems students typically see, often all the way through their senior level computer science courses, are presented in such a fashion that they require no system analysis, little (if any) system design, no testing beyond simple debugging, minimal external documentation, and certainly no hint of maintenance.   They are almost always "toy" problems.   So, even after the experience of an entire computer science curriculum, the student is often not in a position to appreciate the place of software engineering within the discipline of computer science.

This is the computer science maturity paradox.   The students enter the undergraduate program believing computer science is programming and programming is computer science.   They do not have the background or motivation to be dispossessed of this notion and, without a broader understanding of computer science, it is difficult to present software engineering concepts.   However, with each semester that passes, the amount of software engineering that can be added to the program decreases.   Changing any undergraduate program is by necessity a zero sum game and there is already more advanced material which must be saved for the senior year than can possibly be presented.

Finally,   computer science programs tend to have very substantial jargon which must be learned by the student. Unfortunately, software engineering is likewise very terminology dependent.   When the computer science terminology is not in consonance with the software engineering terminology, the confusion can be   substantial. If the students are not sufficiently well grounded in computer science (or software engineering) to be articulate in the terminology then a new jargon, which is in conflict with the first, makes the proper associations of terms very difficult and inhibits learning.

Academic Maturity.

Our students, who rate very high in incoming ACT and SAT scores, are typically about 2.5 on the Perry Scale of cognitive learning. This means that as freshmen they consider the instructor to be all knowing, all disciplines complete, and all knowledge known. [CORN79; CULV82] Studies at other universities indicate this is a universal situation at the freshman level. It is difficult, as you might imagine, to interest this type of student in a discipline where the first tenet is that there are few, if any, other tenets. Students at this level are not comfortable with the study of amoebic topics that are not clearly defined and do not have absolute correct answers.

Until they have the level of academic maturity to be able to cope with ambiguity, incomplete knowledge, and conflicts of reality and theory (about 4.0 on the Perry Scale--see Appendix D), it is difficult to present many of the details of software engineering. In addition to making an overt effort to move the student along the Perry scale, presentations to students low on the cognitive learning scale must be significantly different than those who are more academically mature (e.g., graduate students.) For example, highly structured presentations, with reasonably few conflicts, concrete examples, and chances to practice are much more important to the beginning student than to the more mature student. [CORN79:3]

Another effect of the lack of academic background is that the student is typically not capable of strong analytical thinking. This is reflected in an inability to do mathematical or logical reasoning and an inability to persuasively communicate in oral or written form. The eclectic nature of the software engineering discipline makes this issue even more critical. Thinking, reasoning, and communication skills are the glue that binds together and interfaces the multiple disciplines that converge in software engineering.

Personal and Social Maturity.

The final maturity that is often lacking in undergraduates, especially the freshmen and sophomores, is the personal and social variety. While it is quite possible to be inarticulate, shy, or personally insecure, and still successfully study some disciplines (engineering or computer science???), it is very difficult to succeed in the "social" aspects of software engineering with these warts. Computer scientists have long had a reputation for being somewhat anti-social and unique because of their close relationship with machines instead of people. However, this is not an image that is acceptable for the software engineer.

The major responsibility and interface for the software engineer is to humans, not to the machine. Consequently, the social/personal maturity aspects are as important for the software engineer as for any other service oriented professional. Without this maturity, the user interaction becomes even more difficult and requirements analysis is even more confused. The relationship between analyst and designer, and between designer and implementer are highly dependent upon the individuals' ability to set aside egos and work for the good of the whole. This is a very difficult concept to explain to anyone who has insufficient social maturity to reach beyond the "me."

So Why Not Wait?

Undergraduates typically mature significantly in the three categories we have described by the time they graduate. So, knowing that the maturity of the student is very important in the understanding of software engineering, why not wait until graduate school to introduce the discipline. I suspect that argument was also used forty years ago about computer science and probably many other modern disciplines. The more immature the discipline, the more mature the practitioner or learner of that discipline must be. Unfortunately, the reality is that we cannot wait for software engineering. We can neither have only master's level people able to speak confidently about software engineering topics nor can we wait for the discipline to mature enough to be easily taught to undergraduates. The future has been forced on us by advances in other areas and we cannot look the other way.

Some would propose that the solution to the problem of undergraduate software engineering is simply to wait until the senior year and then present a software engineering course (or even two if you are lucky) [MYNA87] to use the maturity in computer science which has been developed in the first three years. Our experience with this approach has been that it is better than nothing but is woefully inadequate in preparing them to be effective when they meet the demon software crisis the day after graduation. They may learn some of the buzzwords, and perhaps can even adequately use a tool or technique, but it is highly unlikely that they really have a grasp on the fundamental issues of the problem or see enough of the big picture to understand what has befallen them.

Conclusion

The problems involved in teaching a master's degree program in software engineering are just as pertinent for undergraduate coverage of the discipline and are compounded by the significant difference in maturity level between a graduate and undergraduate student. We believe that while an undergraduate software engineering major is not appropriate at this point, it is also unreasonable to attempt to teach software engineering in one course stuck onto the end of a computer science program. Therefore, in order to more effectively integrate software engineering as an aspect of our computer science curriculum, we have attempted to identify the major problems that are unique to the presentation of software engineering topics to undergraduates. We found these problems to be: student deficiencies in computer science experience, academic maturity, and personal/social skills. These deficiencies result in some very subtle problems which must be attended to in any attempt to integrate software engineering into an undergraduate computer science program.

AN APPROACH TO UNDERGRADUATE SOFTWARE ENGINEERING EDUCATION

Introduction

We now feel that software engineering should have a significant role in our undergraduate computer science program. Our goal is to make that role approximately an equal partner with the more traditional software and hardware components of the major. The change in our computer science major has come about gradually and is not completely accomplished; however, it appears we are very close to our goal of producing graduates who have sufficient background in software engineering to go into the Air Force and succeed in the large system development jobs they are typically given. This paper will discuss our current approach to integrating software engineering into the computer science major--it will not attempt to explain the various intermediate steps our curriculum took en route to this final (we hope) form.

This approach is based upon the idea of an education spiral, where each level is built on the previous and the scope is broadened as the spiral climbs. In this case, the base of the spiral, we call it the "overview," is done in the first course in the computer science major. The second level of the spiral is accomplished in a two course sequence in the senior year, which we call the "synthesis." Between these two loops is the "infusion" which allows significant broadening from the first loop to the second. A master's course in software engineering would fit nicely as the third loop of the spiral. One advantage of the spiral paradigm is that it provides iteration of the basics, giving the student a firmer foundation for further work or education. It should be noted that our software engineering spiral is well integrated with similar spirals for the "normal" software and hardware pillars of the major.

The "Overview"

The first course in our major is CS225, Fundamentals of Computer Science. The goals of this course are threefold: 1. present the student with an overview of the computer science discipline and major; 2. provide coverage of the topics outlined in the ACM CS2 1984 recommendations [KOFF85]; 3. provide background and motivation for software engineering. The only prerequisite for this course is an ACM CS1 1984 [KOFF84] type course which gives some experience in structured Pascal programming and problem solving.

When compared with the ACM CS2 recommendations, the unique aspect of this course is the twelve lesson block spent on software engineering concepts. These twelve lessons come toward the end of the course and constitute almost one third of the material covered in the course. This timing and magnitude does several significant things for us. First, it gives the students a very real sense of the importance of software engineering because they tend to judge the importance of a topic by the emphasis it receives within a course. Secondly, it allows us to use the basic computer science concepts presented earlier in the course as a foundation for the software engineering discussions. This is especially effective since these computer science concepts are still very fresh in the minds of the students. Thirdly, this portion of the course uses and builds on the terminology introduced earlier--there is no confusion on jargon because it is presented in a single course and, therefore, must be consistent.

This total and natural blending of software engineering and computer science concepts requires significant orchestration to be effective. In this regard, the book and organization of the course are extremely important. The book we selected, **Advanced Programming and Problem Solving** by Schneider and Bruell [SCHN87], is very true to the ACM CS2 1984 requirements and, therefore, covers software engineering at the "micro" rather than the "system" level [RICH86] we now require. However, this is not as disastrous as it might seem. The book does approach the material from a modified lifecycle perspective which allows us the latitude to expand to the system level using the same lifecycle framework. We assign the lifecycle phase readings from the book but lecture about each lifecycle phase from a system or process level. For example, in the section of the course devoted to implementation, the book discusses normal software product implementation issues like coupling and cohesion. The lectures take the topic to a new plane and discuss the effects of the incremental and traditional approaches to implementation on the product _and_ the process. It is this emphasis on the process and the system that we found missing from the standard CS2 1984 course.

The variation between the reading and the lectures does not seem to present a difficulty to the students because the lectures are ultimately anchored to the readings. Also the lectures are presented at a freshmen/sophomore level and include many examples and references to what they have already accomplished in the course. Although the lifecycle view of system development we provide in the lectures is at a very high level, we attempt to deal in checklists and concrete concepts as much as possible. Consequently, most of the ambiguity and lack of absolutes that make software engineering difficult are hidden from the student.

One aspect of the course which generates numerous very useful examples is the course project. Although it is not large in the software engineering sense (about 2500 lines of Pascal), it is by far the most difficult project they have accomplished. The project is incremental in nature with the definition of each increment being less complete than the previous. This approach gives the student a taste of many things which can be easily and understandably extrapolated to system level software engineering problems. It is this idea of scale which is so very important to the understanding of software engineering. For example, it is always necessary for the student to "maintain" the code written for one increment when he begins to add to it at the next increment. This small taste of maintenance gives them something concrete to relate to during our class discussions on the importance of the requirements analysis and the problems involved with maintaining a large product.

Additionally, we require appropriate documentation as part of the product they produce and this too must be maintained as each increment is designed and implemented.

The syllabus in Appendix A gives a general idea of the structure of the course and we will gladly share more detailed lecture notes and project definition to anyone who is interested. In summary, it is the objective of this course to introduce the student to both the "micro" and "system" level definition of software engineering. It is designed to give a basis from which the problems of scale can be discussed, both in terms of technical computer science and in terms of the management of a non-visible product. [WASS83] We emphasize that the product is important but that the process may be the key to solving the software problem. We also discuss the concept of a software lifecycle and the relationship of various parts of the lifecycle to the software problem. Finally, we stress that the methodological approach to software system development is important, although we obviously do not have time to present a methodology in this course. It is important to remember that this brief overview of software engineering is presented in the context of the entire discipline of computer science.

The "Infusion"

The second stage of the integration of software engineering into the computer science program is perhaps the most difficult to accomplish. The difficulty comes from the required course planning and curriculum control. In this stage, the seeds that have been planted in the "overview" must be nurtured and cultivated. This is done in three parts: introduction of tools and concepts, constant return to basic software engineering concepts and terminology, and the addition of software engineering aspects to exercises and homework assignments. The difficulty comes because, unlike the "overview" and "synthesis" stages, this "infusion" process is not confined to a single course but, of necessity, must involve almost all other courses in the computer science major.

The first requirement is that a consistent set of tools and techniques be introduced and used in the courses following the "overview." In order to do this, a methodology must be decided upon and the components of that methodology directed for use in the appropriate courses. We, for example, have selected a modified version of Structured Analysis/Structured Design (SA/SD) from the Yourdon school. The methodology is not as important at this point as the consistency with which the tools and techniques are used. Because of this methodological selection, we introduce and use data dictionaries, data flow diagrams, structure charts, structured English, Input-Process-Output diagrams, etc. wherever appropriate in our courses. Sometimes the students are required to solve problems using these tools and sometimes the symbology of these techniques is used to define the exercise or problem that the student is to solve in a programming language. This consistent use of the methodological tools puts the student in a position of developing facility with the tools one at a time in a smaller context where they make more sense.

The second aspect of the "infusion" is consistent reference back to the overview of software engineering the students were given in CS225. There is no attempt to extend the "overview" in these courses but we do attempt to reinforce the ideas that have already been studied. Of course, this requires that all instructors be reasonably conversant with the ideas and concepts that have been proffered in CS225. We feel the dividends to be gained from this integration across courses is very significant--certainly significant enough to warrant the investment in time.

The third aspect of the "infusion" of software engineering into our non-software engineering courses is the selection and description of exercises assigned in these courses. As mentioned above, whenever possible a student exercise is written up using the symbology from the appropriate methodological tools. Additionally, instructors are strongly encouraged to require analysis, design, and documentation whenever possible in the exercises they create for the student. We are especially interested in analysis of users' requirements as a part of the graded effort by the student. When possible, multiple turn-ins are made part of the exercise so the designs and user interface information can be checked prior to the implementation of the exercise solution.

It is obvious that this portion of our plan to integrate software engineering into the program is the most costly in terms of coordination among courses and training of the instructors. However, after the initial burden, only minor preventative care will be necessary and the results should continue to be very positive.

The "Synthesis"

The denouement of the software engineering concepts comes in our capstone or "synthesis" sequence. This sequence is a two semester project course called CS453/4--Analysis and Design. In this course, the students combine the concepts, tools, and techniques they have seen as small unintegrated ideas into a single methodology for the solution of a large, "real" problem. This course, more than any other portion of the integration effort, has gone though revision after revision to achieve the maximum effectiveness as a first real experience in software engineering. Our hope is that the next time they are involved in a large software system development effort, it will be significantly simpler because they will have seen the problems before and can fall back on the experience gained in our capstone course. Therefore, we are adamant that this course should take them completely through the development cycle (and into operations and maintenance if possible) for a significant project. This implies that it cannot just be a survey course but must illustrate some complete methodology including both technical and management aspects. (This is the same methodology previously selected in the "infusion" stage.) Of course, this does not preclude the inclusion of a survey of other techniques and methodologies, and as time permits, we attempt to illustrate the other software engineering approaches they may encounter. It is in this course that dividends are paid for the introduction of tools and symbology in previous courses. These experiences not only allow repetition but more significantly, understanding of these techniques. Not having to introduce these tools in the "synthesis" course also allows us more time to study the underlying theory of software engineering and to achieve some depth in several topics. We are very fortunate to have two semesters in which to accomplish this synthesis and we are anxious to optimize their use.

We have looked at a wide variety of different definitions for a project-oriented software engineering course (e.g., [COLL82], [MYNA87], [THAY86], [TOMA87]) but feel that our own experience over the last six years is probably as good as any guidance we can find in the literature. Very briefly, our rules for this course are as follows:

1. The instructor is the most important single element in the course. The instructor will serve as the user, the manager, and the technical advisor.

2. The instructor must have followed the steps through the lifecycle for the project in order to understand the likely pitfalls and to be able to evaluate the student solution and progress.

3. The project must be "real." (Or at least the students must think it is!)

4. For sake of control and consistency, the instructor must be the user. The "user" must provide the students at least a taste of the typical user "cluelessness" and lack of understanding of the requirements.

5. Class time must be set aside for group interaction, technical reviews, and for conferences with the user, manager, etc.

6. Group size must remain small (3-5) so that everyone gets an opportunity to participate in every phase of the development process. Project size can remain significant even with small groups if the project is spread over two semesters.

7. It is important to have automation to decrease the amount of "dog work." Care must be taken that students' urge to "hack" using an automated tool does not obscure the goals of the project. Tools

must be easy to use and not make the project more difficult.

8.   Continued motivation is required, especially when the project runs across two semesters.

9.   A tri-level approach to new concepts is useful: show the concept, let them try the concept on a simple exercise, then have them apply the concept to the term project.

10. The managerial and documentation requirements for the project must be outlined for the student. Examples of previous documentation and management products are very useful.   However, the student must be responsible for the documentation and management products themselves.

11. The project must be iterative enough to allow fall backs and reworks if required.

12. The students must implement at least part of the product so they can see the results (both good and bad) of their analysis and design.

13. A significant portion of the grade must be based on analysis.   This includes requirements analysis, interface analysis, workload analysis, etc.

The syllabi for the two semesters of this course are contained in Appendices B and C. Again, we are happy to share a more detailed definition of the course and its project to anyone who is interested. Portions of the course are now being taken from the master's level modules developed by the Software Engineering Institute (SEI). For instance, we currently use portions of the modules on configuration management and technical reviews. [TOMA86; COLL86] As more modules become available, we will condense portions of them for integration into this course as well. This puts our students in an excellent position to continue on to a master's in computer science or software engineering, or to start a software engineering job immediately after graduation.

Conclusion

Our concern for several years has been that our students are ill-prepared for the jobs they are most likely to encounter immediately after graduation--the development of large software systems. For this reason, we have done considerable work to integrate into our computer science program an appropriate amount of software engineering. We were especially interested in having our students graduate with a reasonable level of experience in "large" system development. Short of a work-study program, which was infeasible for us, the only solution was a project course. Early experience with our project course revealed that the course by itself was not sufficient to give our students the background and experience they needed. The problem of how to inject more software engineering into our curriculum was significant because of the maturity level of undergraduates. After several false starts, we developed the three part plan presented above to integrate the appropriate level of software engineering into our undergraduate program.

Throughout the above description of our integration approach, it should be obvious that we were trying to counteract the undergraduate immaturity problems which we now regard as the single most significant roadblock to introduction of software engineering. Although it is very difficult to quantify our success, we feel that our graduates from this new program will be well prepared to fill a void which has long existed: the requirement for bachelor-level computer scientists who are effective in software engineering jobs. We cannot depend upon the production of graduate degree personnel to satisfy the software engineering needs of the world--this is obvious from the current state of the industry. We think that Peter Freeman said it very succinctly when he wrote: "Given that most computer science majors go to work in industry, we could raise the general level of [software engineering] competence significantly and provide a better base for further professional training if they were better prepared." [FREE86:72] We have found what we think is a very effective method for raising that general level of competence.

Appendix A

Syllabus for Computer Science 225

Fundamentals of Computer Science

LESSON	READING
1 Introduction/Data General	Ch 1
2-3 Computer Architecture	DASM, Compsim
4-5 Data Representation	370-3, App C
6 Disc Assembly code (DASM)	
7 DASM II	
8 Pascal Review	Ch 1, 2, 3 (DG)
9 Control Structure Review	Ch 6, App A (DG)
10 Data Types	Ch 4 (DG)
11-2 Complex Data Structures	13-46; 69-85
13 Abstract Data Types	95-100
14 Record Variants	Ch 4 (DG)
15 Debug and Testing	473-499
16 Test #1	
17-18 Compsim	Compsim
19 Non-text I/O	Ch 8 (DG)
20 File Processing	209-219
21 Software Engineering	Ch 9, handout
22-3 Requirements	Ch 10
24 Compsim 2	
25 Critique of Compsim 1	
26-8 Design I	Ch 11, 12
29-31 Implementation	Ch 13, 14
32 User Interface	
33 Testing	473-499
34 Documentation and Maintenance	Ch 18
35 Test # 2	
36-7 Sorting	Ch 7
38 Searching	
39-40 Algorithm Analysis I	Ch 17
41-2 Computer Science	

Advanced Programming and Problem Solving by Schneider and Bruell

AOS/VS Pascal Reference Manual by Data General (DG)

Computer Simulator Handout (Compsim)

Dinky Instruction Set Computer Assembler Handout (DASM)

Appendix B

Syllabus for Computer Science 453

Analysis and Design I

LESSON		READING
1	Intro/Overview	
2	Developing Large Systems - The Problem	Papers A, B
3	Developing Large Systems - Some Solutions	Papers C
4	Methodologies	Papers D, E
5	Overview of the Methodology	Papers F, G
6	Overview of the Methodology	PRS Ch 1
7	The Analysis Process	PRS Ch 2
8	The Analysis Process	PRS Ch 4
9	Analysis Methods	PRS Ch 5
10	Intro to Structured Analysis	GS Ch 1
11	SA Tools	GS Ch 2
12	Test 1	
13	Data Flow Diagrams	GS Ch 3
14	Data Flow Diagrams	DFD exercise
15	Data Dictionary	GS Ch 4
16	Data Dictionary	DD exercise
17-18	Computer Career Field	
19	Process Logic	GS Ch 5
20	Process Logic	PL exercise
21	Data Definition	GS Ch 6
22	Data Definition	Data Defn. exercise
23	Human Interface	GS Ch 7
24	Human Interface	Papers H, I
25	HW/SW Study	HW/SW Study Handout
26	HW/SW Study	HW/SW exercise
27	Physical System Design	Handout
28	Physical System Design	Phys Sys exercise
29	Project Management Overview	PRS pp 80-88,123-132
30	Test 2	
31	Term Project Introduction	Term Project Handout
32-41	Term Project	
42	Course Wrapup/ Critique	

Software Engineering: A Practitioner's Approach by Roger Pressman (PRS)

Structured System Analysis: Tools and Techniques by Gane and Sarson (GS)

Appendix C

Syllabus for Computer Science 454

Analysis and Design II

LESSON		READING
1	Term Project Debrief	
2-7	Term Project - Part I	P-J pp 225-230
8	453 Review	P-J ch 4,5
9	Intro to SW Design	Prs ch 6
10	Intro to Structured Design	P-J Pref, Forward, ch 1,2
11	Structured Design Tools	P-J ch 3, append. C
12	Design Qualities -	P-J ch 6
13	Design Qualities -	P-J ch 7
14	Additional Design Guidelines	P-J ch 8
15	Test 1	
16	Transform Analysis	P-J ch 9
17	Transaction Analysis	P-J ch 10
18	Packaging/Design Methodology	P-J pp 230-6;273-7, append D,E
19	Implementation	P-J ch 12
20	Implementation	Prs ch 11
21	Optimization/Performance	P-J ch 13
22	Software Quality Assurance	Prs ch 12
23	Test 2	
24	Testing	Prs ch 13
25	Testing	Prs ch 14
26	Installation	
27	Maintenance	Prs ch 15
28	Data Structure Oriented Des	Prs ch 8
29	Object Oriented Design	Prs ch 9
30	Real Time Design	Prs ch 10
31	Test 3	
32-41	Term Project - Part II	
42	Wrapup	

Software Engineering: A Practitioner's Approach by Roger Pressman (PRS)

Practical Guide to Structured Systems Design by Meilir Page-Jones (P-J)

Appendix D

A Synopsis of

Perry's Stages of Intellectual Development [CULV82]

Stage 1: "Students see the world in polar terms of right vs wrong. Absolute right answers exist for everything. Problems are solved simply by following the word of an Authority."

Stage 2: "Students begin to perceive alternate views, as well as uncertainty among Authorities, but account for them as unwarranted confusion among poorly qualified Authorities."

Stage 3: "Students acknowledge that diversity and uncertainty are legitimate, but still temporary, in areas where Authority "hasn't found the Answer yet." They seek relief in hard sciences and mathematics which seem better understood by Authority."

Stage 4: "Students perceive legitimate uncertainty, and therefore diversity of opinion, to be pervasive. They are suspicious of any evidence or authorities opinion."

Stage 5: "Students perceive all knowledge and value, including Authority's, as contextual and relative."

Bibliography

[CANA86]   James W. Canan, *The Software Crisis*, **Air Force Magazine**, May 1986.

[COLL82]   James Collofello, *A Project-Unified Software Engineering Course Sequence*, **Proceedings of the Thirteenth SIGCSE Technical Symposium on Computer Science Education**, 1982.

[COLL86]   James Collofello, *The Software Technical Review Process*, Curriculum Module SEI-CM-3.0, Software Engineering Institute, Carnegie-Mellon University, September 1986.

[CORN79]   J. L. Cornfeld and L. L. Knefelkamp, *Combining Student Stage and Style in the Design of Learning Environments: An Integration of Perry Stages and Holland Typologies*, presented to the 1979 American College Personnel Association Conference, 1979.

[CULV82]   R. S. Culver and J. T. Hackos, *Perry's Model of Intellectual Development*, in **Engineering Education**, December 1982.

[FORD86]   Gary Ford, *Educational Needs of the Software Community*, in **Software Engineering Education, The Educational Needs of the Software Community**, edited by Norman E. Gibbs and Richard E. Fairley, Springer-Verlag, New York, 1987.

[FREE86]   Peter Freeman, *Essential Elements of Software Engineering Education Revisited*, in **Software Engineering Education, The Educational Needs of the Software Community**, edited by Norman E. Gibbs and Richard E. Fairley, Springer-Verlag, New York, 1987.

[GLAS86]   Robert L. Glass, *Software Engineering and Computer Science: How Do They Differ?*, in **Software Engineering Education, The Educational Needs of the Software Community**, edited by Norman E. Gibbs and Richard E. Fairley, Springer-Verlag, New York, 1987.

[KOFF84]   E. B. Koffman, P. L. Miller, and C. E. Wardle, *Recommended Curriculum for CS1, 1984*, **Communications of the ACM**, Volume 28, Number 8, August 1985.

[KOFF85]   E. B. Koffman, D. Stemple, and C. E. Wardle, *Recommended Curriculum for CS2, 1984: A Report of the ACM Curriculum Task Force for CS2*, **Communications of the ACM**, Volume 28, Number 8, August 1985.

[MYNA87]   B. Mynatt and L. Leventhal, *Profile of Undergraduate Software Engineering Courses: Results from a Survey*, Eighteenth SIGCSE Technical Symposium on Computer Science Education, St. Louis, MO, February 19-20, 1987.

[RICH86]   William E. Richardson, *Why Is Software Engineering So Difficult?*, in **Software Engineering Education, The Educational Needs of the Software Community,** edited by Norman E. Gibbs and Richard E. Fairley, Springer-Verlag, New York, 1987.

[SCHN87]   G. M. Schneider and S. C. Bruell, **Advanced Programming and Problem Solving with Pascal,** John Wiley and Sons, New York, 1987.

[THAY86]   R. H. Thayer and L. A. Endres, *Software Engineering Project Laboratory: The Bridge Between University and Industry*, in **Software Engineering Education, The Educational Needs of the Software Community,** edited by Norman E. Gibbs and Richard E. Fairley, Springer-Verlag, New York, 1987.

[TOMA86]   James Tomayko, *Software Configuration Management*, Curriculum Module SEI-CM-4.0, Software Engineering Institute, Carnegie-Mellon University, September 1986.

[TOMA87]   James Tomayko, *Teaching a Project-Intensive Introduction to Software Engineering*, SEI-87-SR-1, Software Engineering Institute, Carnegie-Mellon University, March 1987.

[WASS83]   *A. I. Wasserman and P. Freeman, Ada Methodologies: Concepts and Requirements*, **Software Engineering Notes**, Volume 8, Number 1, January 1983.

Reducing Student Workload in a
Software Engineering Project Course

David Alex Lamb

Queen's University

Kingston, Ontario, K7L 3N6

Abstract. *Software engineering project courses are highly valuable to students, but often require far too much work. This report discusses some methods for reducing the workload for students of such courses while retaining the important benefits.*

1 Introduction

Several universities offer a one-semester course in software engineering where the main work of the course is to build a small system in small teams of students. Typically the students find such a course highly valuable. They learn many things that will be of practical use to them in the workplace, and learn why some of the principles we try to teach them are important.

Unfortunately, most such project courses are a lot of work, even taking into account how valuable they are to the students. This creates several problems. Some students who should take the course avoid it because of the workload. Others take it, but do poorly in other courses because of the time they spend on the project. For many students, the strain of a heavy workload obscures the real lessons they should learn.

This paper summarizes several techniques I have used or plan to use to reduce the student workload in such a course. I have based it on my experiences with software project courses at two universities (Carnegie-Mellon and Queen's), and on discussions with people who have taught similar courses at other institutions. I have embodied some of these ideas in a Software Engineering textbook[1].

Many of these suggestions will appear to be general comments about how to teach such a course. However, in almost everything that follows (including where the course fits into the curriculum, and what I teach in the course) I was motivated by concerns for reducing workload.

2 Courses and Timetables

At first glance, the only apparent prerequisite for a software engineering course is a firm grounding in conventional programming techniques. Carnegie-Mellon used to offer the course in the first semester of third year. However, most students do not have quite enough programming experience by that point; the coding step takes them too long for the benefit they get from it. C-MU eventually moved the course to fourth year; I believe it could be as early as the second semester of third year with the proper prerequisite.

Beyond a general familiarity with writing moderately large programs, I have found three other areas that a prerequisite course should cover.

Modular Decomposition. Without prior experience trying to modularize, students will produce weak decompositions. This means they will have a hard time balancing workload among team members, changing one module without affecting others, falling back to a subset if they run into time pressure, and integrating their final system toward the end of the course.

Specifications. There is not enough time in a short course for the students to both learn and apply precise methods of specifying the behavior of modules (especially formal methods). They can do a reasonable job applying the methods in the project course if a prerequisite course covers the methods themselves.

Coding to a Specification. As with many forms of communication, a student often does not understand how to write a good specification without prior experience in reading and using specifications. Thus prerequisite course should give students experience in coding a module from a specification, and coding a use of a module from a specification. Ideally, such a coding exercise should also drive home a point about information hiding and teamwork. For example, three-person teams could cooperate to write one client of a module and two implementations, and swap implementations without changing the client.

We have created such a prerequisite course at Queen's and offered it for the first time in 1986-7. It requires second year courses in data structures and discrete mathematics (including mathematical logic, functions, relations, and sets). Our first year courses teach the basic ideas of data abstraction and verification.

The results of offering the prerequisite are very encouraging. The students' module decompositions were much better than in previous years, as were their specifications. Our first attempt at teaching the prerequisite neglected to have the students code to a specification. Thus the specifications were still not readable enough. This year's version of the prerequisite will add a coding exercise.

Almost as important as the prerequisite course is what courses the students are taking at the same time. I do not believe there is any way to reduce the workload of a software engineering project course below "high;" the first few times anyone teaches the course, they are likely to give a workload that is *much* too high. Thus it is important that the students not take other high-workload courses in parallel. Other project courses (such as some compiler construction courses) would probably have high workloads, as would a senior undergraduate thesis. Of course, this measure does not reduce the workload; it reduces the adverse consequences of high workload.

At some institutions it might be possible to add a parallel "Software Engineering Laboratory" course. This does not reduce the workload, but might make the credit students get for the course reflect the workload better. For other institutions this option might be politically difficult.

3 Deliverables

An important part of reducing workload is in deciding what the students should hand in. To get the most out of the course, the students should take the project all the way from requirements to delivery – and to maintenance as well, if there is time. Unfortunately, even in a 16-week course there is not enough time to do all we would want; there is even less time in the 12-week semesters we have at Queen's. Thus you must carefully plan what work the students must hand in, choosing deliverables which help the students learn the material of the course while keeping the workload to a manageable level.

You must give the students examples of the documents you want them to hand in. The one document my students still do quite poorly is the module test plan, for which I have not yet worked out a suitable example (I keep thinking naively that the advice "treat it as if it were a system test plan for your module's driver" ought to work, but it doesn't).

3.1 Requirements

The students need a clear description of what they need to produce to have any hope of keeping on track. There is not enough time for them to learn and apply any of the existing requirements specification languages if they are going to build a complete system. All they can do is learn what principles are important in writing requirements.

I have contemplated handing the students a complete requirements document for the system they will build on the first day of classes. In talking with my students, however, I have found that most of them would much rather have more control over the system they produce. Also, doing part of the project for the students works against the "learn by doing" philosophy that I believe is so important in getting across the key ideas of software engineering.

I have had reasonable success in having the students do a user's guide for their system. They can picture what a user would want to know about their system more easily than they can see how to use formal requirements methods.

3.2 Subsets

Most student groups I have seen are overly ambitious in how much they think they can accomplish. To make sure they have *something* to hand in, I insist that they plan their system as a series of subsets. I have them hand in a "Life Cycle Planning" document that describes possible changes to their system, fundamental (unchanging) assumptions, and the series of subsets. If I had more time in the course, I'd have them deliver a subset, then go on to extend it or modify it.

3.3 Design Documents

Different people have different approaches to software design. I teach methods based on David Parnas' principle of information hiding. For preliminary design I have the students write a document that describes the design decisions each module will hide, and what modules will *use* what other modules.[1] For detailed design, the students hand in two documents: a specification for each module, and an "implementation description" where they specify the design details the module hides (for example, that a particular data structure uses a linked list).

These documents are an important part of material the students learn in the course, but they also help reduce workload. A good module decomposition guides the students in dividing the work among themselves, and makes planning integration easier. Ideally, the specifications should reduce work by giving clear descriptions of what each module should do, thus avoiding time lost to confusion and coordination. Since the students still have trouble writing specifications, the module implementation description gives the students *something* to refer to (however flawed from a methodological perspective) if they have trouble with the specifications.

Before we added the prerequisite course, students did a fair job of module decompositions, but it took them a bit too long to decide what to do. With the prerequisite, I believe their module decompositions are now reasonably good, and thus they have an easier time doing the later steps that depend on the module decomposition. The two main pieces of advice I give them to guide their work are

1. Avoid cycles in the *uses* relation between modules, to make system integration and subsetting easier.

2. Don't carry the rule of "make each design decision the secret of one module" too far. If you have several closely related design decisions (such as the meanings of several related commands in a command interpreter) it is reasonable to put all of them in one module, if that combined module would be small enough to make a reasonable work assignment. If you have what appears to you to be a single design decision but the module that hides it looks like it would be much larger than most of the others, find a way to split it up.

Without the prerequisite course, the students did a terrible job of writing specifications. Even with the course, most of their formal specifications are hard to read. We are trying to improve the prerequisite course, but we may never get it to the point where they have enough experience to do a good job of black-box specifications in the project course. I have considered requiring them to write specifications in the "abstract model" style of Figure 1. This is not a proper "module specification" (black box), nor is it a "program specification" (white box), but rather it is somewhere in between. It seems to be easier for the students to handle.

---

[1] *Uses* is a technical term David Parnas introduced. Module X uses module Y if any program that includes module X must include a correct implementation of module Y for X to be considered correct. To a first approximation X uses Y if procedures of X call procedures of Y, but *uses* is not really the same as *calls*.

The secret of this module is the representation of integer sequences. The abstract model of an integer sequence is an unordered set of integers.

```
type IntSeq = ...
```

```
procedure AddSeq(var t:IntSeq; low,high:integer; procedure TooMany);
```

{ Add all the numbers between low and high inclusive to the sequence. That is,

$$\text{final } t = \text{initial } t \cup \{i | low \leq i \leq high\}$$

If there is not room enough in the sequence for all of the numbers in the range, call TooMany, leaving t unchanged. Notice that if $low > high$, you add no elements. }

```
procedure DelSeq(var t:IntSeq; low,high:integer);
```

{ Remove all the numbers between low and high from the sequence. That is,

$$\text{final } t = \text{initial } t - \{i | low \leq i \leq high\}$$

It is not an error if some of the numbers were not already in the sequence. Notice that if $low > high$ you delete no elements. }

```
procedure AllSeq(t:IntSeq; function Each(low,high:integer):boolean);
```

{ Call Each once for each contiguous range of integers in the sequence, in increasing order, until Each returns true or the sequence is exhausted. If the successive values passed to Each are L_i and H_i, $1 \leq i \leq K$, then

$$\forall i : L_i \leq H_i \wedge H_i < H_{i+1} - 1$$
$$\forall i : \forall j \in [L_i..H_i] : j \in \text{initial } t$$
$$\forall j \in \text{initial } t : \exists i \mid L_i \leq j \leq H_i$$

For example, after adding 1, 3, 4, 5, 7, 8, 10, call Each with 1,1; 3,5; 7,8; 10,10. If the sequence is empty, do not call Each at all. }

```
procedure InitSeq(var t:IntSeq);
```

{ Initialize the sequence to empty. Clients must call this for each sequence before applying any other procedures from this module to the sequence. }

Figure 1: Sample "White Box" Specification

With implementation descriptions, the main problem is that the students do not have the judgement to realize how much they need to write. Despite my admonitions to the contrary, they tend to write long pseudo-code descriptions of all the procedures. I try to tell them to write just enough so that, given the specification and the implementation note, any competent programmer should be able to write the implementation they have in mind. For example, with an abstract data type such as a set, you should only need to say "implement sets as a record containing a fixed-size array of elements (sorted in increasing order) and a count of the elements in use". Given the specifications of the set operations, the coding of the procedures should be straightforward.

3.4 Test Plans

I have the students write system test plans, integration test plans, and module test plans. Of the three, the integration test plan is the most important one in reducing their workload. It shows them clearly what modules they have to finish first and gives them a plan for how to work in parallel. The module test plans are important because they will use them during integration to check out individual modules, but doing module-level testing is usually not very hard for senior-level students.

4 Encouraging Good Habits

I believe that the most important reason for teaching software engineering by a project course is that students do not understand why they should follow the principles we teach until they have to apply them. Programming instructors are painfully aware that many students apply stylistic rules only because the graders look for them, and not because the students believe the rules are good in themselves.

Within a project course there are several disciplines that are good for the students to follow, but which many students will not use unless nudged a bit.

4.1 Part versus Whole

Projects of the size I assign typically have ten to twenty modules. I generally do not have the time or patience to grade ten specifications, ten listings, and ten module test plans for each of five or six groups. I have tried two approaches. Originally, I asked each group to hand in all their specifications, listings, and so on, and I would randomly choose one of each for each student. To reduce workload, I recently asked each student to hand in a specification for one module, but advised them to do specifications for all the modules, "for their own good."

As with many similar exhortations, the students ignored me. The result was that the students had no specifications for some modules, and the resulting confusion cost them more time than it would have taken to do the specifications in the first place. Thus I strongly recommend using my original policy of having students hand in specifications for everything, but grading a subset.

4.2 Other Deliverables

In a group project there are several things the team *should* do that they might not do without a push. On the other hand, it might not make much sense to grade them – either because there is no real basis for grading them, or having them graded would get in the way of their real purpose. With each of these items, I insist that the students do them and hand them in, but give full marks for any reasonable attempt.

Minutes. Groups usually cannot remember what decisions they made in previous meetings unless they write them down. I have each person take notes for minutes at at least one meeting, and encourage the students to take minutes at all the meetings.

Walkthroughs. I believe that brief code walkthroughs are a good way to encourage writing readable code. I have each person act as chairperson of a code walkthrough of another person's code, and submit a report of what the walkthrough discovered. The walkthroughs have sometimes discovered problems early enough that students had time to fix them – and sometimes have revealed problems the students chose to ignore, to their sorrow.

One group did a walkthrough of some source printouts rather than compiled listings because one member hadn't finished writing his code yet. For some reason this didn't raise alarms in anyone's mind; eventually at system integration time two other group members had to rewrite this student's code completely.

Logs. I have the students keep logs of the time they spend on the course. They hand in logs each week; my grader scans them for any problems that he thinks I need to be aware of. At the end of the semester they hand in a summary report on how much time they spent on various activities.

The effects of the logs on workload are almost entirely indirect (except for the extra time it takes to keep the logs). Focusing on where their time is going helps some students realize when they are spending too much time on one area, and gives them a better general awareness of how they are using their time. In the long term, looking at the logs shows me how the students are spending their time, which often gives me ideas of how to reduce workload in later versions of the course.

4.3 Meetings

The students must work together, which usually means they must meet – and therefore must run meetings successfully. I give a lecture on running meetings early in the course, give a handout describing how to run a successful meeting, and remind them of how to run meetings a few weeks later.

My students still spend too high a proportion of their time in meetings. Many of them say that the main reason for this seems to be that it takes them too long to make decisions. I am planning on introducing a new system next fall whereby I dedicate some of my office hours to short meetings with each group. Each group will meet with me for 15 minutes each week for me to help them reach decisions. I will have them explain the options they see, and will either guide them in making a decision if I think they are close, or make the decision for them if they are too far from one. I will have to temper any such "help" with the "learn by doing" principle: the students should make most of their decisions themselves.

The system C-MU used when I was there is much better. The instructor rounded up several senior Ph.D. students or staff programmers and had each act as an advisor to one group. This meant each group could get an hour or more each week of personal attention from an experienced programmer. Unfortunately this approach isn't feasible for smaller institutions.

To some people this does not seem like the type of thing a university course should teach. However, most of the students learn nothing about running meetings before they enter such a course, and successful meetings are crucial to reducing the workload of such a course. Thus it is worth spending a half of a lecture or so on this topic.

5   Some Things to Avoid

In some conversations about project courses, other people have made some suggestions for reducing workload that I don't believe are appropriate. This section summarizes these suggestions and my reasons for rejecting them.

- *Use the whole class as one large group, where individual students specialize in one aspect of the course.* Other people, such as   Tomayko [2] , have made this approach work. However, I think that for pedagogical reasons the students should all be exposed to nearly the same experience, which means they should operate in fairly democratic teams where each person does a little of each activity.

- *Appoint team leaders.* Once again this makes sense; a leader can reduce the time the students waste agonizing over decisions. However, few upper-year students (or Master's level graduate students) have the qualities it takes to make effective leaders. I have higher hopes for my plans to meet with the students to help them with decision making.

- *Give the students part of the system.* Some people have suggested giving the students specifications (or even implementations) for some of their modules However, this requires that you give them their module decomposition (or part of it), too; rarely have I seen much similarity between the decompositions the different groups use for the same problem. When I have suggested this to the students, they haven't wanted me to do it; they would rather have more control over (and responsibility for) their own work.

One approach that might work is to give the students skeletons of common modules such as command scanners or menus, and give them the option of using the standard module, modifying it, or writing their own. This is a lot of work for the instructor unless he or she happens to be an experienced programmer; it might require cooperation between people at several institutions to be practical.

- *Don't make the students actually build a system.* Some people observe that getting a system working requires a lot of "grunt work" in coding and testing that doesn't add much to the students' education. However, those last few weeks of putting all the pieces together are crucial for showing the students why all the planning we have them do earlier in the course is valuable.

6 Conclusion and Acknowledgements

Software engineering project courses are valuable but exhausting for the students. A lot of the "grunt work" seems necessary. Improving the quality of such a course involves many years of observing where the students are spending too much effort for the value they get, and trying to reduce the effort they need to spend.

I based most of this paper on experiences teaching Queen's courses CISC422 and CISC838, and would like to thank the students who have taken those course from me for their patience and their suggestions. Margaret Lamb and David Parnas gave me several helpful comments on earlier drafts. An earlier version of this paper appeared as Queen's University Department of Computing and Information Science External Technical Report ISSN-0836-0227-88-206. The Natural Sciences and Engineering Research Council of Canada (NSERC) supported the writing of this report under grant A0908.

References

[1] David Alex Lamb, *Software Engineering: Planning for Change.* Prentice-Hall, Englewood Cliffs, NJ (1988).

[2] James E. Tomayko, "Teaching a Project-Intensive Introduction to Software Engineering," SEI-87-SR-1, Software Engineering Institute, Carnegie-Mellon University (March 1987).

An Undergraduate Course in Software Design

Daniel Hoffman*
Department of Computer Science
University of Victoria

Abstract

While there are many software engineering courses being offered today, there are few that successfully teach software design in a large system context. Many of the courses present good ideas but neglect concrete design techniques and leave the students ill-equipped to actually *do* software design. We describe a course whose focus is the design and use of software modules. The course emphasizes practical module specification methods and provides students with experience in the roles of module designer, implementor, tester, and user. We describe the course content and format in detail and summarize our teaching experience. We conclude with recommendations for standardization in software engineering education.

1 Introduction

Undergraduate software engineering education suffers from an attempt to teach too much breadth. Many courses attempt to span all of the management and technical material that is relevant to the task of building large software systems. The result is that students learn a lot about software engineering issues, but precious little that is directly applicable to software development. More depth is needed and, to some extent, breadth must suffer. According to Peter Freeman

> The experience of the past ten years argues even more forcefully that design must be the integrative knowledge and activity that is the core of software engineering. That part of the content of SEE [software engineering education] must be emphasized and put into effective action [Fre87].

This paper describes an undergraduate course in software engineering focusing on software design. The course teaches the Software Cost Reduction (SCR) method

---
*Research supported by the Natural Sciences and Engineering Research Council of Canada under grant A8067.

[PC86], developed by Parnas and others at the U.S. Naval Research Laboratory over the past 10 years. Our course has grown out of one originally taught by Parnas while at the University of Victoria. The principles on which the course is based are unchanged. Over time, we have made considerable improvements in the format and examples of the course. We have also changed the course to emphasize module design while reducing the time spent on other topics.

The remainder of the paper is divided into three main sections. In Section 2, we describe the software engineering principles and development phases on which the course is based. Section 3 presents a detailed description of the course, including lectures, exercises, and team project, as taught in fall 1987. Section 4 presents our recommendations for a core body of software engineering knowledge, and a summary.

2 The Software Engineering Basis

In this section, we characterize the software engineering problem and describe the principles and software development phases on which the course is based.

2.1 The Software Engineering problem

As distinct from solo programming, we characterize software engineering as multi-person, multi-version programming. Multi-person programming must solve the problems of precise specification of both the complete product and the component programs. Further, the development task must be divided amongst the programmers, and their efforts must be properly coordinated. Multi-version programming involves writing programs that can be delivered in a variety of configurations and that are easily modified as changes occur over time. Finally, software engineering depends on systematic validation to show that the software performs as required. However, we make little use of verification (i.e., program proving) - it has yet to be shown practical.

Despite claims to the contrary [KP85, page 2], software design is difficult. The designer is typically faced with a large number of issues and alternatives, making it very difficult to keep his perspective. The challenge is to find simple solutions to complex problems. Creativity, skill at mathematical modeling, knowledge of the application area, and hard work are required.

2.2 Fundamental Principles

Our approach to solving software engineering problems depends critically on sound basic principles. These principles suggest solutions and provide perspective. They also support productive design reviews: without agreement on basic principles, reviews often degenerate into aimless arguments about programming philosophy.

Our principles are simple to state and remember, though sometimes challenging to apply.

Separation of concerns [Dij76]

The dominant problem in software engineering is complexity. *Separation of concerns* is the decomposition of a problem into independent, or nearly independent subproblems. These subproblems can then be solved directly, or decomposed further. A good software engineer must learn to recognize and reject over-complicated solutions and to deal with the essential complexity using separation of concerns.

Information hiding [Par72]

In large software systems, maintenance costs are commonly high, often exceeding development costs [Boe76]. Even apparently simple changes may be very expensive to implement. *Information hiding* is a systematic approach to design for change based on recording expected changes and encapsulating these changes in separate modules.

Abstraction

When faced with a complex problem, we can use *abstraction*, removing unnecessary features to generate a simpler problem. We then solve the simpler problem and apply the solution to the original version. Of course, an abstraction that eliminates essential parts of the problem is unacceptable. We seek to make the problem as simple as possible - but no simpler.

The central role of documentation

In software engineering, documentation is of paramount importance. Proper documentation distinguishes the hacker from the engineer.

Because documentation plays such an important role in our approach, we describe our approach to documentation in more detail below.

2.3 Documentation Principles

We pay careful attention to the quality of our documentation and attempt to meet the following criteria. Documentation should be complete and correct and so should be structured to make completeness and correctness easy to determine. It must also be easy to change - or it won't remain complete and correct for very long. Since few people read technical documents cover to cover, the documents must be designed for reference use, quickly providing answers to specific questions. Good quality documentation is expensive to produce. It is especially difficult to generate after the development is complete. Therefore we propose documents that are triple-purpose, being used in design, implementation, and maintenance. Initially, they are the medium for recording design decisions and are the focus of an iterative criticism and refinement process. During implementation, the documents tell users what to expect, tell implementors what must be done, and serve as the standard of correctness for testing. During maintenance, the same documents aid in training new staff, support analysis of change, and provide a structure for recording changes.

For the document scheme just described to be effective, a document plan must be developed at the start of the project, with room for all the relevant information. When changes are necessary, both the document plan and the documents themselves must be revised. Milestones and reviews must include documents as well as code.

In summary, our design methods are based upon the central role of these documents. They are, in some ways, more important than the code. Discard the code and keep the documents and you can recreate the code quickly and capably. Discard the documents and the resulting system will be difficult to control and expensive to maintain.

2.4 Software Development Phases

Above, we have described the principles on which our approach to software development is based. Here we describe the software development phases in which these principles are applied. Currently there are two major criticisms aimed at phased approaches to software development. The first is that it is impractical (or impossible) to develop software strictly according to phases, e.g., completing *all* specifications before any coding is done. The second objection is that prototyping is an essential technique in software development and can't be used in a phased approach. These criticisms are based on the misunderstanding that "backtracking" to a previous phase and prototyping are somehow incompatible with phased development. In the article [Roy87, reprint] which introduced the so-called " waterfall model", Royce clearly and specifically advocates the use of both iteration between phases and prototyping. In our own teaching and development we have followed Royce's advice, with good results.

Below we describe the software development phases of the SCR method [PC86].

Requirements Specification

The Requirements Specification [Hen80] describes the required behavior of a system in terms of the observable inputs and outputs of that system. Each input and output is uniquely named and precisely described. To support design for change, expected changes in the system's required behavior and environment are recorded. Since most systems are too large to be implemented by a single person, the development task is decomposed into work assignments called *modules*.

Module Decomposition

The module decomposition is based on *information hiding* [Par72]. For each module, the Module Guide describes the module's *secret* and gives a brief description of the service it offers.

Interface Specification

An interface specification is written for each module describing the services that the module provides, in terms of calls made on, and values returned by the module. Interface specifications are *black box*, expressed without mention of internal data structures and algorithms.

Uses Structure Design

The *uses structure* is an example of what we call a *software structure* [Par74]: a graph whose nodes and edges are associated with software objects. In the uses structure, the nodes are access programs (the calls named in the interface specifications) and there is an edge from access program A to B if the correctness of A depends on the presence of a correct implementation of B. The uses structure is helpful in designing subsettable systems [Par78] and in scheduling integration testing.

Internal Module Design

Program specification consists of choosing the internal data structures, or *module state*, and writing program specifications. For each call supported by the module, a state transition function expresses the value of the module state after the call completes, in terms of the value before the call was made. For calls that return values, an abstraction function expresses these values are expressed in terms of the module state.

Module Test

We make heavy use of scaffolding [Bro75], e.g., drivers and stubs, so that modules can be tested standalone, or nearly so. The ability to effectively test modules in isolation is valuable during integration testing and maintenance.

Integration Test

Finally the modules are tested in combination. The success of integration depends on the ability to quickly determine, for each bug discovered, the module causing the bug.

3 Course Description

In this section, we describe the course environment, the teaching strategy, and the course content and format. We close by summarizing our teaching experiences.

3.1 Course Environment

The Department of Computer Science at the University of Victoria has a young, research-oriented faculty with 15 regular members. Software systems is an important research area in the department, with work ongoing in software engineering, software development environments, programming languages and compilers, and distributed systems. The course described in this paper, *CSC 365 - Software Engineering* (hereafter just '365'), is a required course in the undergraduate curriculum. Prerequisites include *Computer Programming I and II, Discrete Mathematics, Data Structures*, and *File Structures for Data Processing*. Most students have taken courses in computer organization and in digital logic, and many have also taken an operating systems and a basic theory course. Most of the 365 students are computer science majors and are enrolled in the co-op program - a five-year undergraduate program requiring four or five terms of full-time employment. Students typically take 365 after their first or second co-op work term. Their work term experience generally makes them better software engineering students. As well, the course provides valuable training for their remaining work terms. The course has been taught with roughly the same content every spring and fall for the last four years, with an enrollment of 20 - 40 students each term.

3.2 Teaching Strategy

Our approach to teaching 365 is based on the following three themes:

1. Focus on modules, the building blocks of large software systems.

2. Make frequent use of concrete, fully-worked examples to illustrate the lecture material.

3. Use traces when describing module behavior.

Below we describe each of the three themes in more detail.

Although 365 covers all of the software development phases, we emphasize modules: specifically the Module Decomposition and Interface Specification phases. There is not enough time to provide substantial training in all of the phases and we believe that the module-oriented techniques are the most mature and the most readily applicable in employment after graduation. Early in the course, we introduce the following four roles: module designer (i.e., interface specification writer), implementor, user, and tester. We describe the viewpoint and skills appropriate to each role, and require the students to become capable in each role. We emphasize that module designers, implementors, testers, and users can communicate through interface specifications, largely eliminating the need to talk to each other. The notion of implementation "to specification" (i.e., *exactly* to specification) is also emphasized.

In teaching this course we have tried to follow the well-known advice of Kernighan and Ritchie for teaching programming.

> Good programming is not learned from generalities, but by seeing how significant programs can be made clean, easy to read, easy to maintain and modify, human-engineered, efficient, and reliable, by the application of common sense and good programming practices. Careful study and imitation of good programs leads to better writing [KP81].

We have adapted this advice for the design and implementation of programs to that of modules. Before asking students to write interface specifications, we present the best examples available. We then ask them to change these "model" specifications by adding new features. Only then do we have the students write their own specifications. We follow a similar approach when teaching internal module design and implementation.

When discussing module behavior, we have adopted a somewhat novel approach. We wish to be precise and yet avoid discussing module internals - only the implementor is concerned with these. So we describe module behavior in terms of traces, where a *trace* is a sequence of calls, with parameter values, on the module. In our own research, we have used traces in connection with the formal specification method of the same name [BP78,HS86], where logic assertions are used to characterize module behavior on *all* possible traces. Although the trace method is very powerful, considerable skill is required to devise these general assertions. However, it is quite straightforward to describe module behavior for any *particular* trace: such a trace describes a single test case for a module. While test cases are no substitute for specifications, they are very useful for describing particular situations. We use traces for lecture examples, assignments, exams, and module test programs.

3.3   Course Content and Format

In this section, we describe the course lectures, solo assignments, and team project for the fall 1987 offering. The first half of the course emphasizes mathematics and systems fundamentals, and interface specifications. In this training portion of the course, all assignments are completed on an individual basis. The second half presents the software development phases, reinforced by case studies and the team project.

3.3.1   Lectures

The lecture schedule is shown in Figure 1. As we know of no text suitable for the course, we use the papers referenced on the schedule and also supply, online, the code and documentation for several "model" systems. The lectures cover four main topics.

Fundamentals

These lectures provide the necessary mathematics and systems fundamentals. We briefly review the discrete math topics of sets, relations, functions, and graphs, and propositional and predicate logic. We also cover programming language and operating system basics, currently the C language and Unix operating system [Hor86]. We emphasize the importance of the mathematical material - it is useful across application and development environments. We deemphasize the language and operating system choice - a good designer must be prepared to work with whatever language and operating system he is given

Week	Area	Topic
1		Course Overview [Bro87]
	Fundamentals	Logic
	Fundamentals	Logic
2	Fundamentals	The C language [Hor86]
	Interface specification	Modules and interface specifications
	Interface specification	The SCR language [Hof88]
3	Interface specification	The SCR language [Hof88]
	Interface specification	The SCR language [Hof88]
	Fundamentals	The C language [Hor86]
4	Fundamentals	Sets, relations, graphs, software structures
	Interface specification	Evaluation criteria
	Interface specification	The SCR language [Hof88]
5	Fundamentals	The "build" software structure [Fel79]
		MIDTERM
		Review
6	Development phases	Introduction [PC86]
	Development phases	Requirements specification - introduction
	Development phases	Requirements specification - example
7	Development phases	Requirements specification - project
	Development phases	Module Decomposition [Par72]
		Team meeting
8	Interface specifications	The trace language [HS86]
	Interface specifications	The trace language [HS86]
		Team meeting
9	Interface specifications	Traces versus SCR [Hof88]
	Development phases	Uses structure design [Par78]
		Team meeting
10	Case studies	Abstract interface design [Par77]
	Case studies	Device interface module design [B*78]
		Team meeting
11	Development phases	Program specification - motivation
	Development phases	Program specification for C programs
		Team meeting
12	Case study	Example from instructor's consulting
	Case study	T.H.E. system [Dij68]
		Team meeting
13		Review

Figure 1: Lecture Schedule (Fall 1987)

Interface Specification

We put considerable time into teaching students to read and write interface specifications in the SCR language [Hof88]. We begin with trivial modules and progressively increase the complexity, normally presenting complete specifications, rather than "fragments".

Software Development Phases

These lectures motivate the use of phased software development and present the phases described in Section 2.4. Case studies are inserted as is convenient, being careful to cover each phase in lecture before the project teams begin work on that phase.

Case Studies

Although the techniques we teach are designed for large systems, there is not time to complete such a system in a one term undergraduate course. To give students some intuition about large systems, we use case studies, drawn from the literature and from the instructor's academic and industrial experience.

3.3.2 Solo Assignments

The purpose of the solo assignments is to provide training in the basic techniques described above under "Fundamentals" and "Interface Specifications". Over time, we have found that such training is best accomplished with many short assignments, graded and returned very quickly. We issue eight assignments before the midterm. These are normally graded and returned within four days of the due date. Although the load on both students and graders is high, the fast feedback is worth the effort. We carefully design the exercises to make grading straightforward and we accept no late assignments - these seriously impede fast turnaround.

Grades for the module implementation exercises are computed by a test program. The program executes a series of traces on the module, printing the traces and deducting points where the result fails to meet the specification. Since our principal goal is not to teach programming techniques, but rather to convey the concept of writing code "to specification", the pitiless objectivity of the test program is precisely what is needed.

3.3.3 Project

After the training period, culminating in the midterm, the students begin a team project. Project teams (three or four students) are chosen by the students themselves. The primary goals of the project are to give students team experience. We also want to expose them to a software system complex enough to make the value of precise specifications apparent - in a small system it may still be easier to read the implementation code rather than the specifications. Each team is assigned a "consultant" - either the course instructor or a grader, who meets with the team weekly for an hour. For this project the instructor and graders developed a solution before the student teams began work. Although this approach is labor intensive, it is very beneficial. The instructor learns the application *very* well and hones his abilities with the techniques he is teaching. Also, the solution may be useful later. For example, the project for the spring 1988 offering consists of enhancing the instructor's fall solution, by adding a screen interface and several other features. Over time, the instructor's solutions have developed into a collection of "model solutions", valuable for demonstration purposes.

3.4 Teaching Experiences

In this section, we discuss our experiences with teaching 365, briefly review other presentations of the SCR method, and discuss the use of tools in software engineering education.

Overall, our experiences with teaching 365 have been very positive. We have been able to convey sophisticated software engineering principles and concrete design and specification techniques to students with relatively little software development experience. Despite the heavy work load in fall 1987 (between the exercises and project there were 15 graded assignments), student course evaluations were extremely positive. We have found that students badly want to learn a systematic approach to large systems development. This came as somewhat of a surprise - we had expected to meet more resistance to techniques that inevitably delay the start of coding.

We have encountered two main difficulties. The first is that, while our students are capable programmers, their discrete mathematics skills are inadequate. Although the prerequisite courses cover the necessary topics, the students are not comfortable with modeling software problems using relations and graphs. They are familiar with predicate logic, but lack confidence in translating from prose to logic. Our curriculum committee is now in the process of increasing the discrete mathematics requirement from one to two terms. We will welcome this change.

Our second problem is more fundamental and concerns the difficulty of software design. Consider the four roles emphasized in the course: module designer, implementor, tester, and user. While the designer role requires skill in specification writing, the remaining three require only specification reading. We have been very successful in teaching students to read specifications. Much to our surprise, even weak students learn to read and reliably answer questions about relatively complex specifications. Teaching interface design, as expressed in a module specification, has been much harder. As noted above, the lack of discrete mathematics skills causes some difficulties, but the real problem is deeper. We have found that few students can clearly visualize the service a module should offer, record this vision in a specification, and then refine the specification until it is of good quality. The required combination of talent, taste, and patience is, not surprisingly, rare. These experiences have led us to believe that effective software development must maximize the skills of the relatively few good designers we will be able to train. To do so requires both widespread recognition of roles such as those named above and agreement on a relatively small number of specification languages, the basis for communication between designers (specification writers), and implementors, testers, and users (specification readers).

In addition to the undergraduate teaching described above, we also teach the SCR method once a year at the graduate level. We spend more time on the Requirements Specification and Module Decomposition phases, attempt more ambitious projects with larger teams, and pursue research topics as well. Other courses based on the SCR method are currently taught at Queens University in Ontario, Canada and have been taught at the Wang Institute [Wei87]. We have also taught short courses to industry in Canada, the United States, and Europe. Typically these are five-day courses, with roughly the same lecture schedule as in the undergraduate course, fewer exercises, and a very small team project. These short courses have been well received, despite the large amount of material covered in such a short time.

We conclude this section with a brief discussion of the use of tools in software engineering education. For 365, we depend on only the most rudimentary tools: an editor and a programming language supporting separate compilation (so that students can develop modules independently). As we have been careful to make the course programming language independent, the choice of language has been based more on local conditions than software engineering principles. We currently use the C language because our hardware runs Unix and C is the "home language". The module support in Modula2 (or Ada or CLU or Turing or ...) would certainly offer some benefits, and we may eventually switch. While we try and show students how software tools (e.g., make [Fel79]) can be useful, we feel it is crucial *not* to make tools a major focus of the course. If the students understand software engineering principles and techniques, they can acquire tool skills quickly enough on the job (while getting paid for it). After all, the key to gaining productivity through tools is knowing what to do with them! However, we have found that in the graduate software engineering course, tool building makes an excellent software development project. Using software engineering methods to build software development tools has been a continuing theme of that course.

4 Recommendations and Conclusions

4.1 The Need for Standardization in Software Engineering Education

By Computer Science standards, software engineering is not a new field. The research literature is extensive and considerable practical experience has accumulated. The lessons of the OS/360 project [Bro75] are now over 20 years old. Yet, there is no standard for what constitutes the fundamental concepts and techniques (hereafter, "the core") of software engineering. When a student says he has taken a software engineering course, he provides us with no new information - there is not a single concept or technique that we can be sure he has learned. This situation is in direct contrast to other areas in Computer Science. There is basic agreement on what belongs in a course on data structures and algorithms, programming languages, or formal languages. Although there are numerous software engineering textbooks, many of good quality, they are broad, describing the nature of the field without establishing the core. Nor is the research literature of any help. The *IEEE Transactions on Software Engineering*, for example, publishes articles on virtually every Computer Science topic from artificial intelligence to computational complexity, leaving readers wondering exactly what software engineering really is.

The lack of agreement on the core has been very damaging. There is little cumulative effort in software engineering courses. Such courses are typically "home grown", depending entirely on the skill and experience of a particular instructor. As a result, these courses vary wildly in quality and are not easily taught by other instructors. Further, until a core is established, there is no firm foundation for tool building - there is simply no way to know what techniques the tools should support.

While the contents of the core must be driven by the needs of industry, it is clearly the educator's task to craft it. The raw material is present in the published research and industrial experience. What is lacking is agreement on what is essential versus merely useful.

> In one sense, everything known about software or computers is knowledge that may some day be needed by a designer in order to make a decision; it is the overall task of SEE [software engineering education] to winnow out the most relevant of this mass of information and make sure that the software engineer has access to it [Fre87].

We believe that the focus of the core must be on programming in the large; in our terms: Requirements Specification, Module Decomposition, and Interface Specification. Module implementation and testing are already handled well under data structures, algorithms, and programming methodology. Briefly, the key aspects of the core as we see it are:

Sound principles

The core must be based on sound software engineering principles, such as separation of concerns, abstraction, and information hiding.

Systematic documentation

Systematic documentation, primarily specifications, is essential to controlling development and maintenance costs.

Phased software development

While recognizing potential improvements due to alternative techniques, it seems clear that large software projects will be based on a phased development approach for some time to come.

Methodology and programming language independence

The core must be defined independently of any particular programming language and software development method. Otherwise the core will be neither widely accepted nor generally applicable.

Maintenance orientation

It has long been known that maintenance costs dominate the total cost of large software systems. The core must be oriented towards reducing these costs.

4.2 Summary

We have described a successful software engineering course emphasizing software design. The course teaches sound software engineering principles, and demonstrates them on concrete examples. We have focused on the roles of module designer, implementor, tester, and user. Precise interface specifications are an essential part of this course, as they are the communication medium on which these roles are based. Thus, we put considerable effort into training students in practical interface specification techniques. We have argued the need for a well-established core body of fundamental software engineering knowledge. We have also argued that this core should emphasize software design and specification and be independent of any particular programming language and development methodology. Naturally, in our course we teach this core as best we can. We *have* achieved programming language independence, but certainly not methodology independence. Clearly more discussion is needed to establish this core.

Acknowledgements

The ideas of David Parnas have influenced every aspect of this course. We would also like to thank the students of CSC 365, for showing us how to teach software engineering, and the referees, whose comments led to substantial improvements in this paper.

References

[B*78] K.H. Britton et al. A procedure for designing abstract interfaces for device interface modules. In *Proc. of the Fifth Intl. Conf. on Software Engineering*, IEEE, March 1978.

[Boe76] B.W. Boehm. Software engineering. *IEEE Trans. Computers*, c-25(12), December 1976.

[BP78] W. Bartussek and D.L. Parnas. Using assertions about traces to write abstract specifications for software modules. In *Second Conference of the European Cooperation in Informatics*, Springer-Verlag, 1978.

[Bro75] F.P. Brooks. *The Mythical Man-Month*. Addison-Wesley, 1975.

[Bro87] F.B. Brooks. No silver bullet - essence and accidents of software engineering. *IEEE Computer*, 20(4), April 1987.

[Dij68] E.W. Dijkstra. The structure of 'THE'- multiprogramming system. *Commun. ACM*, 11(5):341–346, May 1968.

[Dij76] E.W. Dijkstra. *A Discipline of Programming*. Prentice-Hall, Inc., 1976.

[Fel79] S. Feldman. Make - a program for maintaining computer programs. *Software - Practice and Experience*, 9(3), March 1979.

[Fre87] P. Freeman. Essential elements of software engineering education revisited. *IEEE Trans. Soft. Eng.*, SE-13(11), November 1987.

[Hen80] K.L. Heninger. Specifying software requirements for complex systems: new techniques and their applications. *IEEE Trans. Soft. Eng.*, SE-6(1):2–13, January 1980.

[Hof88] D.M. Hoffman. *Practical Interface Specifications*. Technical Report DCS-75-IR, University of Victoria, Department of Computer Science, 1988.

[Hor86] R.N. Horspool. *C Programming in the Berkeley Unix Environment*. Prentice-Hall Canada, 1986.

[HS86] D.M. Hoffman and R. Snodgrass. Trace specifications: methodology and models (accepted for publication). *IEEE Trans. Soft. Eng.*, 1986.

[KP81] B.W. Kernighan and P.J. Plauger. *Software Tools In Pascal*. Addison-Wesley, 1981.

[KP85] M.J. King and J.P. Pardoe. *Program Design Using JSP - a Practical Introduction*. Macmillan Publishers Ltd., 1985.

[Par72] D.L. Parnas. On the criteria to be used in decomposing systems into modules. *Commun. ACM*, 15(12):1053–1058, December 1972.

[Par74] D.L. Parnas. On a 'buzzword': hierarchical structure. In *Proceedings of the IFIP Congress 1974*, North Holland Publishing Co., 1974.

[Par77] D.L. Parnas. *Use of Abstract Interfaces in the Development of Software for Embedded Computer Systems*. NRL Report 8047, Naval Research Laboratory, 1977.

[Par78] D.L. Parnas. Designing software for ease of extension and contraction. In *Proc. of the Third Intl. Conf. on Software Engineering*, pages 264–277, IEEE, 1978.

[PC86] D.L. Parnas and P.C. Clements. A rational design process: how and why to fake it. *IEEE Trans. Soft. Eng.*, SE-12(2):251–257, February 1986.

[Roy87] W.W. Royce. Managing the development of large software systems. In *Proc. of the Ninth Intl. Conf. on Software Engineering*, IEEE, 1987.

[Wei87] D.M. Weiss. Teaching a software design methodology. *IEEE Trans. Soft. Eng.*, SE-13(11), November 1987.

Software Tools at the University:
Why, What and How

Laurie Honour Werth
Department of Computer Sciences
University of Texas at Austin

Abstract

The Computer Sciences department is currently involved in various tool technology transfer activities including the use, development, enhancement and evaluation of CASE software as class projects, and a software engineering laboratory for the synthesis of software. Industry cooperation efforts include continuing education courses, beta testing, and joint projects in which university and industry personnel share hardware and software as well as expertise. These endeavors are described briefly and a short synopsis of benefits, problem areas and some possible solutions provided.

Why Should Universities Teach Software Tools?

It is not immediately obvious that universities *should* play a role in the transfer of tool technology since their traditional role is as a purveyor of timeless ideas, rather than volatile physical entities such as software tools. However, tools are not just productivity enhancers which allow an individual to do more in a given period of time, but they are also materializations of ideas and algorithms which allow qualitative improvements in the solutions the tool user produces.

Word processors, spreadsheets and text editors are examples of software tools which make this kind of quantitative improvement in productivity. Academic computer scientists and their students need productivity improvement as much as any organization, but it is hardly sufficient justification for tools to appear in the curriculum.

A more promising aspect of software tools is that tools raise the level of abstraction, and provide a rich environment of ideas for manipulation. Students use tools to suppress low level detail so that they can concentrate on the higher level concepts which they are trying to understand or illustrate. In some sense algorithms are the "theorems" of computer science, and tools, which are the embodiments of these algorithms, allow students to reduce their cognitive load to permit higher levels of conceptualization. It is these characteristics of software as a logical rather than physical entity and as an embodiment of ideas in the discipline that make it a unique type of artifact. Software represents that unique blend of science and technology which sets computer science apart from its sister disciplines of mathematics and electrical engineering. The complexity of modern computer science demands their use.

For example, CASE tools such as Teamwork™ or Excelerator allow students to draw data flow diagrams more easily in the same way a word processor allows them to write a paper more easily. The graphics interface makes it easier to draw more beautiful pictures, but at the same time, the consistency checking reduces the amount of time needed to insure that design principles have been followed and simultaneously teaches principles which may not yet have been mastered.

Graphics are increasingly used in many areas of computer science because diagrams aid clear thinking and improve communication of ideas. CASE tools make the physical process easier while providing error checking and enforcing discipline. At walkthroughs, time does not have to be spent to check level balancing or to verify data dictionary elements; students can concentrate on the system being represented. By not having to worry about the syntax, they can concentrate on the semantics.

But more than that, graphical specification techniques are a higher level of information exchange than text. Diagrams improve communication where more than one person needs to understand the system, making it easier to understand, modify or communicate this information to others. Diagrams graphically illustrate thinking at various levels of abstraction. These are stronger reasons why tools are important at the university.

Similarly, a system such as Smalltalk provides for and enforces object oriented programming. Smalltalk also provides students with a rich environment of ideas about programming and the programming process. Software engineering concepts have been materialized. Students are freer to concentrate on the product, rather than the process.

Inside computer science, the area of software engineering benefits especially from tool use. The following discusses laboratories, courses, and industry cooperation in tool technology transfer at the University of Texas at Austin.

Software Engineering Laboratories

The University of Texas is fortunate to have received hardware and software grants which provide a rich software engineering laboratory environment. Grants from Hewlett-Packard and IBM have provided much of the hardware and basic software. Funding from AT&T for a rapid-prototyping lab has been enhanced by grants and discounts from software vendors. Some departmental money was provided, together with software contributions from faculty and student projects.

HP Laboratory

Several grants from Hewlett-Packard provided twenty-four Bobcats (HP9000 model 320 and 350) networked together in two laboratories. These Motorola 68020 based workstations have 8MB memories, high resolution monitors and 130MB hard disks. Major software provided by HP on these systems includes HP-UX (UNIX®), HP and X windowing environments, the HP AI workstation software, Prolog, Pascal, Fortran and graphics software. Teamwork™ (from Cadre through HP) and Smalltalk were added recently. A faculty member contributed Tmycin, a Tiny version of Emycin. The lab also supports four Artificial Intelligence classes, as well as occasional use by several other classes and individual projects. The size and quality of these workstations has substantially enhanced Software Engineering education at the University. This laboratory has been so successful that it is being expanded to include additional workstations, printers, and HP/third party software.

Microcomputer Laboratories

Several grants from IBM provided thirty-five IBM XT's . Each has 512K of memory, a printer, two floppy disk drives and a hard disk. Index Technologies provided copies of Excelerator/RTS (real time system) and documentation through their Education Grants Program. Support tools such as word processors, database management systems, spreadsheets, graphics (GKS, display and presentation) packages, and prototyping tools have been acquired.

Project management, expert systems and other artificial intelligence software are currently being added. These machines are now older technology; they provide access to the large pool of MSDOS software but performance and human interfaces are a problem in the use of modern software Engineering tools. The lab is being used for Data Structures and File Structures classes, as well as Software Engineering and individual projects.

Some Macintosh software, such as HyperCard and project management tools, have been added. A department network connects many of these machines and gives access to campus-wide network which includes university mainframes. If current proposals are successful, this lab will be expanded.

AT&T Rapid Prototyping Laboratory

Software for this laboratory is intended to be component elements from which software engineering tools can be synthesized. These component sets come in several levels of resolution. The lowest useable level is a collection of information handling, analysis, and display modules. The next levels incorporate larger units of functionality such as directed graph editors or CAD packages, and intelligent database interfaces. The highest level is a set of tools for each of the functions of software engineering such as requirements analysis, test generation, etc.

While much of this software is available in the PC laboratory, powerful software generators which run on VAXs and/or SUNs are also available. Though there is not enough equipment for class use of these tools, Gandalf (1985), Cornell Program Synthesizer, IDL Toolkit and others are being used effectively by undergraduate and graduate students for individual and Honors projects. PAISLey (Zave, 1987) is on order and Refine™ has been loaned by Lockheed Corporation for joint projects.

Software Engineering Class Projects

According to a recent survey (Werth, 1987), few universities use tools as class projects and only a handful of universities provide automated tools for students; yet these are two of the most fundamental ways to encourage future tool development and utilization. The following discussion covers only the tool aspects of the classes and does not completely detail course activities. Possible activities promoting CASE tools at the university are illustrated.

Enhancing Tools

CS 373 is a standard undergraduate project-oriented software engineering class, limited to graduating seniors. This fall semester, 1987, students used CASE software, installed on the HP workstations. Teams were formed and used Teamwork™ on their first, small "shake down" group project. The rest of the semester was spent developing an enhancement to Teamwork using its ACCESS features. Students selected their own features, based on their earlier experience, then documented and implemented their systems following Fairley's (1985) project outlines: System Definition, System Requirements Specification, three Design Documents, User's Manual, Test Plan, Project Legacy and Project Notebook.

Several projects to improve Teamwork's Data Dictionary facility provided additional reports and consistency checks to make walkthroughs and data flow diagram development easier. Teamwork provides some examples of ACCESS routine use and these became our library of reusable code. While students did not have to understand the entire system, the exercise did motivate the desirability of object-oriented design, project databases and good documentation.

One team provided a project management capability which printed management reports including a Gantt chart marked as of the current date, and a log report which produces warning messages as to the number of days remaining before reviews/completion, last modification date of database objects, etc. Reports were based on Teamwork status label information which included scheduled, actual, and review dates, together with author information and comments for all database objects.

The most ambitious project, an interface prototyper, used finite state diagrams from Teamwork's real-time capabilities and the ability to attach UNIX® files to all components of the diagrams. A Screen Design Language defined in BNF and a powerful menu system were developed as part of this excellent project.

All teams made extensive use of UNIX® scripts and utilities such as Make, Lint, ADB and Curses. Mail and login/out logfiles demonstrated the effectiveness of good team communication. One team used SCCS, but it was decided that it was not reasonable to use within our constraints. (RCS was not available.) The most time-consuming problems resulted from coding in C. Major organizational problems came from the necessity to keep the latest version of code, documentation and system models (databases) in a central location so that team members could access them regardless of the workstation presently being used.

Students worked incredibly hard and produced unusually professional products, due in large degree to the improved hardware and software environment together with the motivation which resulted from working in a realistic environment.

Developing Tools

Earlier Software Engineering classes have successfully developed a variety of static and dynamic analysis tools for testing software, designed for future software engineering classes. As above, teams analyzed, designed, implemented, tested, maintained and documented their products based on the Fairley text.

Students were having trouble parsing the Pascal programs, so a partially complete recursive descent parser for Pascal was given to the teams. This unplanned aid actually gave students valuable experience with maintaining another programmer's code and the parser was big enough that the methodology tools were immediately seen as valuable. The recursive parser is also one of the most popular reuse items. More parsers are needed in and for various languages if students are to be able to concentrate on tool development within tight time constraints.

The author had earlier supervised the development of several semesters worth of software engineering tools at another university after it became obvious that the only way students would have tools would be for them to develop their own. A data flow diagram/data dictionary/structure chart tool was one of the most successful. Done before commercial systems and graphic terminals were available, the entire class cooperated on the project. Database, database and data dictionary reports, consistency checking, and graphics teams designed and implemented a UNIX®-based, dumb terminal/line printer oriented system which could be expanded to graphics terminals by future classes. Again, realism prompted superior work on the part of the students.

Software tools make excellent class projects. Not only is motivation high, but students become their own users, reducing instructor effort and the application domain knowledge learning curve. It introduces students to the concept of customer interaction as well as encouraging them to produce their own tools in the future.

Evaluating Tools

During the spring '86 semester, students evaluated three commercial systems as part of their work in the software engineering course. The original system design was developed using PCSA on IBM XTs. After entering their designs into both Excelerator on the IBM XTs and Team*work* on the HP workstations, an evaluation form based on Weiderman et al (1986) was developed and completed by the students. This information was presented through HP's University Associates Program to provide feedback for the Team*work* developers and to aid other universities in attendance to incorporate similar programs.

The spring '85 Software Engineering class used a VAX version of USE.IT™ developed by HOS (Hamilton, 1983; Martin, 1984)) for the analysis and design of their class project, a Pascal interactive debugger. There were some problems due to an incompatible version of the operating system, as well as to the formalisms required. The present, interactive version of USE.IT™ on the SUN's is extremely easy to use and viable for class use when sufficient hardware becomes available.

Having the student teams evaluate each other's projects has become standard part of the software engineering class. Teams are given the user documentation, several trouble report forms and an evaluation form for one or more class projects. Several of the reported problems are repaired to provide maintenance experience. Peer pressure yields rapid repairs and reenforces the importance of user satisfaction.

(Re)Using Tools

Projects from Software Engineering classes are saved for reuse by later classes. The spring '88 class will use existing projects for an enhancement exercise. The summer '88 class, emphasizing project management, will "manage" earlier projects among other activities. Such reuse reduces the amount of coding needed for students, especially during the short summer semester.

Graduate students have reused software from classes and individual projects, in combination with lab tools, to produce a variety of products ranging from test data generators to intelligent interface packages.

Current plans call for the fall '88 Software Engineering class to combine both the front end capabilities of Teamwork, Excelerator or IDE, with the rich program development environment provided by Smalltalk to implement an object oriented system project.

ParcPlace Smalltalk on the HP machines is already in use by the Programming Languages classes.

Industry Cooperation

The University of Texas at Austin is involved in numerous activities which combine university and industry capabilities. Many graduate students work for MCC and other companies in the Austin area, while others are supported by research grants on various military and industrial projects. Adjunct faculty teach classes, including Software Engineering. The following examples illustrate ways in which software engineers and practitioners can work together to promote tools in software engineering education.

Continuing Studies Courses

The Office of External Affairs administers two types of industrial education courses: "short courses," open to the general public and taught mainly on the UT-Austin campus, and "in-house seminars," taught on a contract basis to employees of single companies, usually at the industrial site. Twelve short courses taught during 1987-88 included two in Software Engineering, both of which featured tool demonstrations and one of which included hands-on Teamwork lab in the afternoon. In-house courses are primarily in software engineering, and can include use of a faculty member as a consultant to work with a pilot project to apply concepts taught in the course.

The department has established a self-supporting staff position to handle the organization and publicity for the industry courses and other events such the departmental Computer Science Research Review presentation for industry. Future efforts will include the use of electronic mail for transmitting information to industry about the department's activities and a series of video conferencing short courses from the UT-Austin campus to other cities.

Beta Testing and Benchmarking

USE.IT™ has been incorporated into several student and computation center projects, as well as being used by the spring '85 Software Engineering class. The current SUN version (now marketed by Sema Metra in France) was beta tested at UT last spring. This had the side effect of one graduate student being hired by the vendor.

Wasserman (1986) provided a copy of his IDE™ (Interactive Development Environment, part of his Unified Support Environment (USE), methodology). An earlier version was incorporated into several projects including an inventory database for the hardware maintenance staff. The latest version, which includes extensive analysis/design and rapid prototyping facilities, is being evaluated in projects by several students. When the HP version becomes available, IDE will be used in the Software Engineering classes.

The Teamwork™ project was successful in encouraging dialog with HP staff members and student evaluations of the system were forwarded to the company at the end of the semester. Students were intrigued that the company might want to hear their opinions and were surprisingly mature in their comments.

Training Materials

The University of Texas and Lockheed Austin Division (LAD) cooperate on a number of research efforts, including software engineering, real-time systems and artificial intelligence projects. A recent approach to technology transfer featured the use of a university faculty member to develop training materials for a Lockheed product, AdaCraft (an APSE for the Rational1000). The course, taught several times in Austin, Los Angeles and Houston, includes slides and hands-on exercises, and is an outstanding example of mutually beneficial university-industry cooperation.

Collaborative Projects

Currently, plans are underway for another collaborative effort with Lockheed using Refine™ a knowledge-based programming environment developed by Reasoning Systems, Inc. Refine, a very-high-level, wide-spectrum executable specification language based on research in program synthesis, is currently implemented on Symbolics 36xx and Sun-3 systems. Two faculty members have attended a short Refine training course held at Lockheed. Next semester, graduate students and Lockheed employees will undertake evaluation and application projects such as the development and implementation of an interpreter for a high level domain-oriented language, using a Refine license loaned by Lockheed.

Advantages of Using Tools the University

Benefits of incorporating tools into the university software engineering curriculum are discussed in terms of instructional improvements and university-industry cooperation advantages.

Instruction

Assigning tools as projects provides students more motivation than the usual yet-another-throw-away-programming-project, since there is a possibility that someone will actually use the program. Students learn to think tools, and tend naturally to automate their tasks in the future. Besides the improvements in productivity and learning, the improved realism of enhancing a large system is exciting and provides relatively painless maintenance training.

Graphics tools are particularly helpful in teaching the Structured Analysis/Structured Design methodologies. Grading data flow diagrams and structure charts is as difficult as grading programs. Consistency checking by the tool aids learning in the same way the compiler teaches programming language syntax. This frees up walkthrough time to concentrate on the strengths and weaknesses of the system rather than correcting the diagrams. There was measurable improvement in the mastery of the requirements and design techniques using automated tools.

Outstanding software and documentation is inspiring for students, while some of the less desirable products make nice counter-examples to use when students slide into sloppy work. Relying on good, or even poor, software products, more quickly drives home the fundamental motivation for good software engineering practices.

Task oriented commercial software provides valuable experience for students who have been trained on generic systems such as UNIX®. Productivity improvements impress students who have not been encouraged to share or automate their work. The course attracts a noticeable higher quality student, more motivated to learn software engineering.

Industry-University Cooperation

Hardware and software vendors benefit from having their products exposed to both university and industry students. The liberal discounts are a measure of the value which vendors place on this service.

Industry cooperation such as beta testing provides realistic experience for students, with the corresponding benefits of knowledgeable user feedback for the vendors. Faculty benefit from "real-life" experience, while companies benefit from a fresh perspective. Collaborative efforts such as those with Lockheed, HP, and Sema Metra help faculty keep up to date on industry practice.

Technology transfer discussions inevitably lead to discussion of attitudinal issues. Having experienced the benefits of commercial software, students are largely over the "Not Invented Here" hurdle. They also have a broader foundation upon which to make their decisions as to the relative costs and benefits of various products and product features.

Some Problems

Problem areas are divided into those concerned with the expense of acquiring and using tools, and those related to the educational aspects of applying tools at the university.

Expenses

Class-sized numbers of automated tools and their hardware are expensive. Space for labs is a crucial issue on this, as on most, campuses. Manpower is needed to install, maintain and proctor software and hardware.

While many vendors offer educational discounts ranging from 25 to 85 percent, CASE software can be so expensive that it is still out of reach. Outright grants of software and/or hardware are needed, but the cost of supporting equipment, documentation and supplies must be covered as well. Security must be considered. Permission to duplicate manuals is important in reducing costs. Evaluating, ordering, installing and learning new software consumes valuable faculty and student time, as well as money.

Training

Many systems are not designed for a student environment and do not provide features such as team/file security or on-line tutorial documentation and examples. Networking provides unfortunate realism as teams struggle to work together on systems designed as individual workstations. Incompatibility between tools remains a major problem throughout software engineering.

Classes share each lab, so usage is heavy and diverse. The system administrator requires patience, as well as all-knowing powers to anticipate and recover from frequent crises, student enthusiasms, software/hardware bugs and deficiencies. Tutors or proctors remain a unknown luxury at this point, however students help each other. Focusing on the team as an instructional unit in the lab improves learning substantially, still the noise for small group "tutoring" can be a distraction to the other students.

Faculty, teaching assistants and system administrators must be trained to use the system as well as the students. Yet, few training materials exist.

Some Solutions

A few inexpensive, practical ideas for getting started with tools, garnered from our experiences at the University of Texas at Austin, are outlined below.

Expenses

Many software tools can be acquired by grants and educational discounts for relatively small amounts of money, especially for the micro-based systems. Students benefit from writing their own tools as projects.

Hardware is a more serious issue. Many schools already have some IBM or other PC equipment from previous grants or have access to some through the computation center. Microcomputers acquired for introductory classes are sufficient to start. Getting started with windowing tools provides an important foundation for more complex software later. Students with Macintosh experience pick up Smalltalk easily, for example.

As workstations become more common, their price will come down, but VAX's and the expensive graphics terminals are not likely to become readily available for Software Engineering labs. Vendors may become more responsive to university needs, as software engineering tools represent a large, broadly-based market.

Money earned from industry training courses can represent a major source of funding for both hardware and software.

Manpower is the major difficulty for overburdened faculty members. The cheapest source of labor is students. ACM, IEEE, Upsilon Pi Epsilon or other student groups may be willing to undertake a service project to aid the department. They may also find it profitable to offer an inexpensive training course for other students on general support tools such as word processors, spreadsheets, UNIX®, etc. Some students find the experience of installing/testing software enough fun to do it for free. Many of them are knowledgeable enough to be extremely helpful, especially in such areas as micros and public domain software.

A central, up-to-date, database, describing CASE software capabilities, configuration requirements, sources, evaluations and current prices is a high priority item everyone, not just universities. SEI is working in this area, but results are not yet forthcoming.

SRA sells a Software Engineering Automated Tools Index and NTIS and DACS have catalogs of available Federal agency software. DeMillo (1987) contains a gold mine of information on testing tools. For micro software, of course, read the appropriate review publications. Project management and 4GLs are well documented at bookstores and computer shops.

Training

Faculty must have ready access to the necessary hardware and software. The learning curve is greatly reduced, if one simply begins with a task that needs doing and applies the tool. Graphic interfaces do make tools easier to learn. Menus and on-line help get one started without reading the manual. As needs arise, new features are explored.

A consistent (Macintosh/windowing) interface between tools makes succeeding tools easier to learn. Soon it is a puzzle how one ever got along without them. Productivity improves and the time can be spent on other more important tasks, such as learning to use more tools or producing training materials. The main ingredient is time. The most important part is to get started; the rest will take care of itself.

Producing training materials is the next most time consuming, though companies are becoming attuned to this problem. One expert system vendor includes all of their training materials including video tapes, in their university discount package. UNIX® publications (UNIX®/World tutorials) and books (Kernighan & Pike, 1984; Thomas, Rogers & Yates, 1987) are widely available. Relatively inexpensive documentation is available from USENIX, if your organization is a member.

Charette (1987) and James Martin, (1985, 1987) discuss software tools and provide examples of commercial systems. Other texts are underway and should begin to appear. Barstow (1984) and special issues of journals (IEEE) provide classroom material.

Student research papers are a beginning. The Software Engineering Institute (SEI) produces excellent training modules for Software Engineering. Hopefully, a Software Tools module will appear soon.

Exercises and examples are in short supply. Jim Tomako's class notebook, describing an extensive Software Engineering class project, is available from SEI. Wiener and Sincovec's text (1984) has a spelling checker, while Zelkowitz (1979) and Myers (1978) have some small design examples. Hatley and Pirbhai (1987) have several real-time examples. The problem set for the Fourth International Workshop on Specifications and Design (1986) are possibilities and make it easier for students to read research articles which use them as examples. Large case study systems, especially those documented to existing standards, are needed. The Software Engineering Institute plans to release an "Ada artifact," which can be used for enhancement/maintenance projects for classes.

Conclusions

Software Engineering courses include experience using, developing, enhancing and evaluating CASE tools, improve learning and provide students with the background required to meet the changing needs of software technology. Software Engineering Laboratories can furnish a learning environment for both students and local industry personnel in the form of short courses with hands-on laboratory experience. Joint industry-university projects combine the best of both world to acquire, evaluate, incorporate, and produce training materials for CASE tools quickly and effectively. These processes establish communication between university and industry and enhance the transfer of tool technology in both directions.

It is important for large universities such as the University of Texas, to take a role in the transfer of tool technology. Software tools have shown their value in the university, but some may feel such activities detract from their role as research centers. It is important for us all to work to reduce the gap between concept and practice. Basic research is needed, but research must include experimentation and application of results.

Effort is needed from universities, government and industry to overcome shortages of money, time and training materials. Universities provide a broad background of knowledge and a generic perspective on the problems and solutions. Industry provides motivation and practical experience, as well as the means to study, measure, and evaluate tool technology effectiveness. High costs and common budget problems can be reduced by sharing hardware and software resources, as well as by combining education and experience.

Quantitative productivity and qualitative cognitive improvements make software tools well worth the effort. But, integrating software tool technology is a long, slow process. If universities don't start now, they may fall irreparably behind due to the difficulty of the task and the speed with which the field is advancing.

Bibliography

Barstow, D., Shobe H. and Sandewall, E. *Interactive Programming Environments.* McGraw Hill, 1984.

Charette, R. N. *Software Engineering Environments: Concepts and Technology.* McGraw-Hill, 1986.

DeMillo, R., W. McCracken, R. Martin, and J. Passafiume. *Software Testing and Evaluation.* Benjamin Cummins, 1987.

Excelerator. "A Guided Tour of Excelerator," Index Technology Corporation, 101 Main Street, Cambridge, MA 02142.

Fairley, R., *Software Engineering Concepts*, McGraw-Hill, 1985.

Gandalf. *The Journal of Systems and Software.* Vol. 5. No. 2. May 1985. (entire issue).

Hamilton, M., and S. Zeldin, "The Functional Life Cycle and its Automation: USE.IT." *The Journal of Systems and Software*, Vol. 3, 1983, pp. 25-62.

Hatley, D. and I. Pirbhai. *Strategies for Real-Time System Specification.* Dorset House, 1987.

Interactive Development Environments, Inc. (IDE/USE) 150 Fourth Street, Suite 210. San Francisco, CA 94103.

Kernighan, B. and R. Pike. *The UNIX Programming Environment.* Prentice-Hall, 1984.

Martin, James. *System Design from Provably Correct Constructs.* (USE.IT) Prentice-Hall, 1984.

Martin, James and Carmen McClure. *Diagramming Techniques for Analysts and Programmers.* Prentice-Hall, 1985.

Martin, James. *Recommended Diagramming Standards for Analysts and Programmers: A Basis for Automation.* Prentice-Hall, 1987.

Morgan, R. and H. McGilton. *Introducing UNIX™ System V.* McGraw-Hill, 1987.

Myers, G. *Composite/Structured Design.* Van Nostrand Reinhold, 1978.

Problem Set for the 4th International Workshop on Software Specification and Design. *ACM SIGSOFT Software Engineering Notes.* Vol. 11 No. 2, April 1986 or in conference proceedings, April, 1987.

Refine™. Reasoning System Inc. 1801 Page Mill Rd. Palo Alto, CA 94304.

Team*work*™ and PCSA™. Cadre Technologies Inc., 222 Richmond Street, Providence, RI 02903.

Thomas, R., L. Rogers, and J. Yates. *Advanced Programmer's Guide to UNIX™.* Osborn McGraw-Hill, 1986.

Warren, W. and R. Snodgrass. *A Tutorial Introduction to Using IDL.* SoftLab Document, Computer Science Department. University of North Carolina, Chapel Hill, NC. October, 1985. Entire issue, SIGPLAN Notices, December, 1987.

Wasserman, A. I., P. A. Pircher, D. T. Shewmake & M. L. Kersten. "Developing Interactive Information Systems with the User Software Engineering Methodology." *IEEE Transactions on Software Engineering,* Vol. SE-12. No. 2, February 1986.

Weiderman, N. H., Habermann, A. N., Borger, M. W., and Klein, M. H. "A Methodology for Evaluating Environments." *Proceeding of the ACM SIGSOFT/ SIGPLAN Software Engineering Symposium on Practical Software Development Environments,* 1987.

Werth, L. "Survey of Software Engineering Education."*ACM SIGSOFT Software Engineering Notes.* Vol. 12 No. 4, October 1987.

Wiener R. and R. Sincovec. *Software Engineering with Modula-2 and ADA.* John Wiley, 1984.

Zave, P. "Salient Features of An Executable Specification Language." *IEEE Transactions on Software Engineering,* February 1986.

Zelkowitz, M., A. Shaw, and J. Gannon. *Principles of Software Engineering and Design.* Prentice Hall, 1979.

Selected References to Software Engineering Tools

CASE Technologies issue. IEEE Software. Vol. 5. No. 2. March 1988.

Gray, D. "A Microprocessor Development Environment based on the Amsterdam Compiler Kit, Emacs and Unix. SIGCSE Bulletin, Vol. 19 No. 4, December 1987.

Henderson, P. (Ed.) *Proceedings of the ACM SIGSOFT/SIGPLAN Software Engineering Symposium on Practical Software*

Development Environments. SIGPLAN Notices. Vol. 19 No. 5, May 1984.

Henderson, P. (Ed.) *Proceedings of the ACM SIGSOFT/SIGPLAN Software Engineering Symposium on Practical Software Development Environments.* SIGPLAN Notices. Vol. 22 No. 1, January 1987.

Houghton, R. "Software Development Tools: A Profile." IEEE Computer, May 1983.

Houghton, R, and D. Wallace. *Characteristics and Functions of Software Engineering Environments: An Overview.* ACM SIGSOFT Software Engineering Notes. Vol. 12. No. 1, January 1987.

IEEE *Conference on Software Tools.* IEEE Computer Society. April 1985.

Miller, E. *Tutorial: Automated Tools for Software Engineering.* IEEE Computer Society Press. November 1979.

Multiparadigm Languages and Environments issue. *IEEE Software.* Vol. 3 No. 1, January 1986.

Porcella, M., P. Freeman and A. Wasserman. *Ada Methodology Questionnaire Summary.* ACM SIGSOFT Software Engineering Notes, November, 1982.

Requirements Engineering Environments: Software Tools for Modeling User Needs issue. IEEE Computer. Vol. 18. No. 4. April 1985.

Riddle, W. and L. Williams. Software Engineering Workshop Report. ACM SIGSOFT Software Engineering Notes, Vol. 11 No. 1, January 1986.

SOFTFAIR II. *A Second Conference on Software Development Tools, Techniques, and Alternatives.* IEEE Computer Society Press. December 1985.

Software Productivity Consortium. 1880 Campus Commons Drive, North Reston, VA 22091. (703) 391-1823. Newsletter and technical reports.

Software Engineering Automated Tool Index, Software Research Associates, San Francisco, CA 1986. $93.

Specifications issue. IEEE Software. Vol 2. No. 2, March 1985.

Waguespack, L. and D. Haas. "A Workbench for Project Oriented Software Engineering Courses." Proceedings of the SIGCSE Bulletin, February 1984, pp. 137-145.

Wasserman, A. *Tutorial: Software Development Environments.* IEEE Computer Society Press, 1981.

Repositories for Public Domain Tools

Computer Products Support Group, National Technical Information Service, 5285 Port Royal Rd, Springfield, VA 22161 (703)557-4763. Directory of Computer Software PR-261/595, Federal Software Exchange Center PR-383/595, Software Tools PR-784/595, free. 1987 Directory of Computer Software PB87-143236 $48.

Data & Analysis Center for Software. RADC/COED, Griffiss AFB, NY 13441-5700, ATTN: Document/Dataset Ordering. DACS Newsletter (free), DACS Information Packet (free), Software Life Cycle Tools Directory $35.

Software Exchange Program, GSA(CF), 2 Skyline Plaza (11 Floor), 5203 Leesburg Pike, Falls Church, VA 22041 (703) 756-2610.

Computer Software Management and Information Center, 112 Barrow Hall University of Georgia, Athens,GA 30602 (404)542-3265. Searches free, catalog $25. Educational discount.

A SCARCE RESOURCE IN UNDERGRADUATE SOFTWARE ENGINEERING COURSES: USER INTERFACE DESIGN MATERIALS

Laura Marie Leventhal and Barbee T. Mynatt
Computer Science Department
Bowling Green State University
Bowling Green, Ohio   43403

ABSTRACT

A recent survey by Leventhal and Mynatt (1987) has suggested that user interface issues have become one of the major topics in undergraduate software engineering courses. In their view, this emphasis potentially presents numerous difficulties for the software engineering educator. In particular, issues of instructor training and availability of suitable materials arise as problem areas. In order to more effectively incorporate user interface concepts into undergraduate software engineering courses, a compact body of material has been developed. This body of material incorporates both practical guidelines to interface design, and discussion of a major theoretical issue in interface design. The material is described in some detail, and observations about its usefulness are included.

INTRODUCTION

A recent survey by Leventhal and Mynatt (1987) has indicated that user interface issues have become one of the major topics in undergraduate software engineering courses. Leventhal and Mynatt suggest that this trend is a surprising one for several reasons. First, courses in cognitive psychology and human factors, the two fields most closely allied with user interface design, are not typically included in computer science curriculum at either the undergraduate or graduate level. One can infer that software engineering educators themselves thus may be ill-prepared to teach issues of interface design. Secondly, the area of user interface receives very limited or no coverage in most software engineering texts currently on the market. Thus software engineering educators are challenged to find appropriate materials outside of the usual textbook sources. In short, software engineering educators appear to be focusing substantial attention on a topic which has few support materials and for which they themselves have little formal training.

At Bowling Green State University we have developed an approach to teaching user interface issues which appears to be quite successful in the context of undergraduate software engineering education. In developing our approach, we have had two primary goals. First, the students need the "how to" to be able to design an effective user interface. Second, we felt that the students should also have an understanding of some of the underlying theoretical issues in interface design to provide a theoretical framework for the pratical applications. These two goals were set in the context of limited instructional time in our software engineering curriculum. To attain both of these goals in the limited time available, we have developed a body of materials which focuses on a single practical guiding principle and a single theoretical issue. This has allowed us to introduce students to concepts of interface design without compromising other aspects of our course curriculum. The level of the materials is intended to be appropriate for senior-level computer science students. In addition, the materials are relatively compact and require no more than three hours of instructional time for coverage.

The remainder of the paper is organized as follows. First, the undergraduate software engineering course at Bowling Green State University is briefly described to provide an example of a "typical" software engineering course. The major topics covered in the course and the role of user interface issues in the course are discussed. This is followed by a description of the "how to" portion of the materials and of our techniques for incorporating them into the classroom setting. Third, the theoretical framework component of the approach is described. It should be noted that the materials described in this paper are described only in concept. An educator who wishes to use the materials will find the necessary references in the references section. The discussions of the approach are followed by our observations of the effectiveness of its use. In addition, an annotated bibliography of some general readings in the area of user interface design is included.

THE UNDERGRADUATE SOFTWARE ENGINEERING COURSE AT B.G.S.U.

The undergraduate software engineering course at Bowling Green State University is offered by the Computer Science Department, which is housed in the College of Arts and Sciences.

The course is a senior-level, one-semester course, consisting of lectures and team projects. Each team typically consists of 4 to 6 students. The object of the team projects is to complete a real software development project for users from the university community. The projects pass through all phases of the software development cycle. The class lectures parallel and support the evolution of the projects. Thus the major topics covered include requirements analysis, user interface design, preliminary design, detailed design, integration and coding, and testing. User interface design is presented prior to preliminary design. The students are required to design the user interface of their team's project before completing the preliminary design of the system. Approximately fifty-percent of the class grade is drawn from performance on the projects. The remaining portion of the grade is based on performance on small exercises and the examinations.

The undergraduate software engineering course is described more completely in Bickerstaff (1985). This reference also includes a list of the various projects undertaken by the classes up to 1985.

COMPONENT 1: A "HOW TO" GUIDELINE FOR USER INTERFACE DESIGN

Several books have recently appeared which present practical guidelines for interface design. These guidelines are based, when possible, on empirical research (cf. Shneiderman, 1980; Shneiderman, 1987; Brown, 1988; Smith and Mosier, 1984; Sime and Coombs, 1983). However, these books are much too extensive for use in an undergraduate software engineering course. As an organizing principle, our presentation focuses on only one guideline: *the type of user and the type of interface should match*. To expand on this principle, we point out that different types of interfaces and different types of users exist. When these types are correctly matched, the user interface is more likely to be successful than if the types are incorrectly matched.

Types of Interfaces. The types of interfaces which are presented include menu-driven (also called "menu selection"), form fill-in, direct manipulation and command language. These interfaces can be distinguished by the amount of information which is presented to the user at any one time, the amount of data entry required and the degree to which the interface structures the user's task.

In a menu-driven interface, the user is presented with all of her/his current alternatives. The user may make a choice among the presented alternatives. Thus, in a menu-driven interface, the user's task is structured by the sequence of menus that are presented. Menu-driven interfaces are commonly found in application software for personal computers. In a form fill-in interface, the user is reminded of the type of information which is required through the presence of field labels. However, the user is required to remember the appropriate format of each response. Form fill-in interfaces are commonly used in applications that require large amounts of data input.

In direct manipulation interfaces, objects in the task environment are represented as visual objects (icons) on the screen, rather than solely as textual information. To perform actions in a direct manipulation interface, the visual objects are manipulated by the user. Direct manipulation interfaces are most easily implemented with the use of a pointing device, such as a mouse, to select and manipulate the icons. Many video games are examples of direct manipulation interfaces. Direct manipulation interfaces reduce memory demands because objects from the task environment are presented. However, alternative actions currently available are not easily represented as icons, and tasks sequences are not structured.

In a command language interface, all of the information
originates with the user. The user must know what alternative
commands are currently available, and must select and enter the
appropriate command. The user must structure the task. Command
language interfaces appear frequently in settings which require
direct communication with an operating system.

Table 1 summarizes some characteristics of the four
different interface styles.

Table 1

SUMMARY OF THE CHARACTERISTICS OF FOUR
DIFFERENT INTERFACE TYPES

Type of Interface	Characteristics
Menu-Driven	- Current alternative actions are present - Minimal data entry required - Appropriate where limited alternatives available - Structures the user's task - Easy to learn - Easy to remember - Reduces errors

Form Fill-in	- Field labels prompt user for data entry
	- User typically must know format of data
	    be entered
	- Appropriate when extensive data entry
	    required
	- Structures the user's task
	- Requires moderate learning
	- Fairly easy to remember

Direct Manipulation	- Represents objects in task environment icons - Presence of icons provides memory aid - Tasks are performed by manipulating ic - Does not structure the user's task - Easy to learn - Easy to remember - Reduces errors
Command Language	- User must know available commands - User enters command to initiate action - Does not structure the user's task - Hard to learn - Hard to remember - Errors are easy to make - Can be extremely flexible and powerful

Types of Users. Users can be differentiated by the amount of experience they have had with computer software. Broadly speaking, three levels of user experience can be identified: limited or no experience; experience which is on-going, but is occasional or intermittent; and extensive experience. These levels can be translated into three types of users: novice, intermittent and frequent.

Matching User Types and Interface Types. The effectiveness of an interface can be measured by five major types of variables: ease of learning, likelihood of user errors, speed of use, degree of user satisfaction and preference, and user knowledge retention. In an interface which is effective, users will easily learn and remember how to operate the interface. They will also have high performance levels and favorable aesthetic responses.

The types of interfaces which are effective for the three user types differ in terms of the effectiveness measures listed above. Novice users seem to be best served by systems which offer only a few options which can be easily learned and remembered. Interfaces which limit the number of possible user-generated errors seem to enhance performance for this type of user, as well. Menu-driven interfaces which offer a small number of logically organized items appear to be most appropriate for novices. In addition, novice users are aided by unambiguous way-finding information, which tells them where they are in the menu structure and how to return to some initial and "safe" configuration.

Intermittent users appear to respond best to interfaces which are internally consistent. Internally consistent interfaces are easily learned by this type of user. In addition, the error and speed performance of intermittent users seems to be considerably enhanced by consistent interfaces. For these reasons, menu-driven or form fill-in interfaces seem to be most effective for such users. In particular, intermittent users are best served by menus or forms which are logically organized, readable, and orderly. Across a system's interface, the menus and forms are more effective if they are consistently organized and displayed.

Frequent users typically need little cuing from the interface. In addition, they are not satisfied with interfaces which slow down their interactions with the computer. These users appear to find form fill-in or command language interfaces to be most effective. However, even this type of user is aided by consistency in form layout, field formats, command syntax and command names.

The relationships between user types and direct manipulation interfaces are not well-understood at the current time. Little empirical research on this issue has been performed. However, Hutchins, Hollan and Norman (1985) have speculated about some of the features of direct manipulation interfaces which might affect their appropriateness for different types of users. The basic guideline and explanation presented here are discussed more fully in Mynatt (in press).

Presentation of the "How To" Guideline. Our basic
guideline and an explanation are presented to the students as a
combination of lectures and examples. Examples from the students'
experiences are usually readily available. For instance, all of
our students are familiar with software for the Apple MacIntosh.
This style of software can be used to illustrate the concepts of
menu-driven and direct manipulation interfaces. Following
presentation of user interface design issues in class, the
students are required to explicitly design and implement the
interface for their projects according to the principle of
matching interface to user type. A preliminary design of the user
interface (on paper) is handed in and evaluated before the
interface is implemented. When possible, an implemented version
of the user interface (a prototype) is completed and evaluated
before the coding of the functional portion of the project begins.
The user interface is evaluated again during the final grading of
the project.

COMPONENT 2: A THEORETICAL FRAMEWORK FOR UNDERSTANDING USER INTERFACE DESIGN

Component 1 of our approach to teaching user interface desig
issues focuses on a practical guideline and stresses the interplay
between the interface characteristics and the type of user. In
the second component, a fundamental theoretical issue in user
interface design is presented and discussed. The issue is: *why
user expertise level is a critical factor in interface design.*In
order to address this issue, we focus on differences between more
and less expert users and how increasing expertise may affect
one's interaction with an interface. In particular, we emphasize
that people at different expertise levels experience identical
stimuli differently (cf. Kaplan, Gruppen, Leventhal and Board,
1986). Stated another way, expert, novice, and intermittent user.
not only work more effectively with different interfaces, but
actually experience identical interfaces differently. Differences
between users of different expertise levels are especially evident
from two aspects of experience: perception and preference. (Not
that although these differences in perception and preference
affect of ease of learning, performance, and satisfaction levels,
a discussion of the interaction is beyond the scope of this
presentation.)

**Perception: Experts, Intermittent Users, and Novices
"See" Differently.** Numerous studies of expertise have
suggested that acquiring expertise results in changes in
perception within the domain of expertise. That is, experts and
novices have fundamental differences in pattern recognition.
Patterns which correspond to meaningful and important objects may
be different for the two groups.

One indication that expert and novice perception differs
arises from the various experiments which have been done using a
technique developed by deGroot (1965). In this type of
experiment, experts and novices are each shown stimuli from their
area of expertise for a short time. The stimuli are presented in

both meaningful and random patterns. Following the exposure, the subjects are to recall or reconstruct the stimuli. In typical results from this type of experiment, novices perform the recall/reconstruction task at about the same low level for both the meaningful and random stimuli. The experts, by contrast, perform well with the meaningful stimuli, but perform at about the same level as the novices with the random stimuli. This pattern of results is quite robust, having been demonstrated in the domains of chess (deGroot, 1965; Chase and Simon, 1973), volleyball (Allard and Starkes, 1980), basketball (Allard, Graham and Paarsalu, 1980), and programming (McKeithen, Reitman, Reuter and Hirtle, 1981).

These results can be interpreted in terms of differences in perception. In the case of the meaningful patterns, experts "see" the stimulus in terms of meaningful objects. In the random stimulus case, there are no meaningful patterns and the experts are forced to deal with each component of the stimulus as an individual object. Novices see both stimuli as equally random and demonstrate the same levels of performance. For example, expert programmers see patterns and groupings in meaningful source code which aid them in recalling the code at a later time. When expert programmers look at random, meaningless code, they see no patterns and can recall very little of the code. Novice programmers, on the other hand, do not see patterns in either the random code or even in the meaningful code. Their recall is equally poor for both sorts of stimuli.

Preference: Experts, Intermittent Users, and Novices Like Different Types of Stimuli. Studies inside and outside of computer science suggest that what experts and novices like, within their domains of expertise, tend to differ (see Berlyne, 1971, for a review). In computer science, Leventhal (1987) presented expert and novice programmers with programming problems and partial programming solutions. The subjects were asked to provide preference ratings for the problems and solutions. She found that the experts were more likely to base their preferences on the programming problems and the novices were more likely to base their preferences on the programming solutions. In addition, experts tended to like items which were informationally rich and complex, while novices tended to like items which were well structured.

The Critical Role of Expertise in Interface Design. Given these differences in perception and preference, one may then infer why user expertise level plays such a critical role in the determination of an appropriate interface. The reason is that two users of different expertise levels will probably experience an identical interface differently. An interface is appropriate for a given user if that user is able to effectively perceive meaningful objects in the interface and if the user likes the interface. A second user may find the same interface ineffective, by virtue of their expertise level, if they are unable to recognize critical objects in the interface or if they do not like the interface.

User expertise plays a second critical role in interface design as well. Users and designers of interfaces typically have different levels of experience, relative to computer use. Designers are "super" expert users of interfaces. Based on their super-expertise, designers may look at an interface and see meaningful objects and beauty in the interfaces that they design. A less expert user may see only random chaos in the same interface. In other words, a designer may design an interface which (s)he experiences as being effective, while users may find the same interface useless.

The difficulty of the designer's task is further complicated because the two processes, perception and preference, operate "automatically". They are uncontrollable processes which cannot be turned on and off at will. As a result, designers cannot trust their own responses to interfaces to accurately reflect the responses of users. A designer simply cannot regress to a lesser expertise level, thus a designer cannot use her/himself as an accurate judge of an interface (cf. Zajonc, 1980; Kaplan and Kaplan, 1982).

Presentation of the Theoretical Issue. In order to convince software engineering students of perceptual changes which accompany increasing expertise levels, a deGroot-type reconstruction experiment is reproduced in class. In particular, the meaningful and random programs developed by McKeithen, et al. (1981) are presented to the class. Following the presentation of each stimulus, the students are asked to write down what they saw. Then the stimuli are reshown and the students grade the accuracy of their reconstructions. Not surprisingly, the students find that their performance in the random-program condition is noticably worse than their performance in the meaningful-program case. They are able to see for themselves that their performance is degraded when the stimulus does not contain meaningful patterns.

Following the experiment, the students are told that novice computer scientists would have about the same level of performance on each of the two types of programs. This difference in performance is explained in terms of differences in recognition. They, as experts, are able to recognize meaningful patterns in the meaningful program case. Such recognition helps them reconstruct the meaninful program relatively accurately. Novices in both cases, and experts in the random case, see no meaningful patterns and have no assistance in reconstruction.

In order to show students that differences in a person's expertise level may also affect what they like, students are reminded of experiences in which they were experts and experiences in which they were novices. For example, many Bowling Green State University computer science students have extensive experience with the UNIX operating system. They report a high level of enjoyment in the use of this operating system now, but typically remember an extreme dislike for the system during their initial exposure.

Convergence Between the Practical Guideline and the Theoretical Issue. Both the practical guideline and the theoretical issue echo a similar theme: the expertise and experience of the user is a critical factor in the success of any interface. For our software engineering students, the practical guidelines suggests some ways that user expertise and interface type may be matched. The theoretical issue explains not only why the same interface may work for one user and not another, but also stresses that the students' own expertise level must be taken into consideration during interface design.

EFFECTIVENESS OF THE USER INTERFACE MATERIALS

The materials we have outlined here appear to be effective in our undergraduate software engineering course. Although we have made no systematic attempt to measure effectiveness, student feedback has been positive. Students often initially feel that the user interface design is "just another programming problem". Following the presentation of this material, they appear to recognize that interface design is a special type of problem. In the development of their software projects for real users, students actively seek user responses to interfaces following this discussion. They also seem to be willing to incorporate user suggestions and feedback into their interfaces. In addition, students who have worked in an industrial setting report that the material clarifies difficulties which they have had in understanding the lack of appreciation from users of some system they have helped to develop.

CONCLUSIONS

From the perspective of a software engineering educator, several challenging questions remain. Most critically, our work in this area raises questions of what other interface design material could or should be incorporated into undergraduate software engineering curriculae, and possibly into the undergraduate computer science curriculae in general. Should we provide more (or fewer) interface design guidelines? Should we provide more (or less) coverage of relevant theoretical topics? How should textbooks handle the coverage of user interface design? Should user interface design become a more prominent issue in earlier computer science courses? Is is possible (desirable) that user interface design should be a topic of a separate course?

REFERENCES

Allard, F., S. Graham, S. & M.E. Paarsalu. (1980). Perception in sport: Basketball. *Journal of Sports Psychology*, 2, 14-21.

Allard, F. & J.L. Starkes. (1980). Perception in sport: Volleyball. *Journal of Sports Psychology*, 2, 22-33.

Berlyne, D.E. (1971). Aesthetics and Psychobiology. New York: Meredith Corporation.

Bickerstaff, D.D. (1985). The evolution of a project-oriented course in software development. ACM SIGCSE Bulletin, 15, 13-22.

Brown, C.M. (1988). Human-Computer Interface Design Guidelines. Norwood, NJ: Ablex Publishing Corporation.

Chase, W.G. & H.A. Simon. (1973). Perception in chess. Cognitiv Psychology, 4, 55-81.

deGroot, A.D. (1965). Thought and Choice in Chess. The Hague: Mouton.

Hutchins, E.L, J.D. Hollan & D.A. Norman. (1985). Direct manipultion interfaces. Human-Computer Interaction, 1, 311-338.

Kaplan, S.& R. Kaplan (1982). Cognition and Environment: Functioning in an Uncertain World. New York: Praeger.

Kaplan, S., L.D. Gruppen, L.M. Leventhal & F. Board. (1986). The Components of Expertise: A Cross-Disciplinary Review. Ann Arbor, The University of Michigan.

Leventhal, L.M. & B.T. Mynatt. (1987). Components of typical undergraduate software engineering courses: Results from a survey. IEEE Transaction on Software Engineering, Se-13, 1193-1198.

Leventhal, L.M. (1987). Perception of Software Quality: Aesthetics and Expertise. Unpublished doctoral dissertation The University of Michigan, Ann Arbor, MI.

McKeithen, K.B., J.S. Reitman, H.H. Reuter & S.C. Hirtle. (1981) Knowledge organization and skill differences in computer programming. Cognitive Psychology, 13, 307-325.

Mynatt, B.T. (in press). An Introduction to Software Engineering with Student-Project Guidance: Prentice-Hall.

Shneiderman, B. (1987). Designing the User Interface: Strategi for Effective Human-Computer Interaction. Reading, MA: Addison-Wesley Publishing Company

Shneiderman, B. (1980). Software Psychology: Human Factors in Computer and Information Systems. Cambridge, MA: Winthrop Publishers, Inc.'

Smith, S.L. & J.N. Mosier. (1984). A Design Evaluation Checklist for User-System Interface Software. (NTIS AD A158 599). Bedford, MA: The MITRE Corporation.

Zajonc, R.B. (1980). Feeling and thinking: Preferences need no inferences. American Psychologist, 35, 151-175.

ANNOTATED BIBLIOGRAPHY

Apple Computer (1987). _Human-Interface Guidelines: The Apple Desktop Interface._ Reading, MA: Addison-Wesley Publishing Company, Inc.

(This book presents the philosophy of the Desktop Interface and describes the guidelines and standards needed for someone developing an Apple Desktop Interface. It presents general design principles which deal with topics of metaphors, direct manipulation, use of recognition, consistency, abstraction of commands, user control, feedback, users' mistakes, stability, aesthetic properties, and graphical communication. Specific standards are discussed for each of the characteristic parts of the Apple Interface.)

Baecker, R., & W. Buxton, (Eds.) (1987). _Readings in Human-Computer Interaction:_ A Multidisciplinary Approach. Los Altos, CA: Morgan Kaufmann Publisher, Inc.

(This book focuses on the importance of the user interface in computer system design, from a multi-disciplinary perspective. The book includes research articles, case studies and a bibliography.)

Brown, C.M. (1988). _Human-Computer Interface Design Guidelines._ Norwood, N.J.: Ablex Publishing Corp.

(Has not been personally reviewed by Leventhal or Mynatt. Included based on the title.)

Gardiner, M.M., & Christie, B. (Eds.) (1987). _Applying Coginitive Psychology to User-Interface Design._ New York, NY: John Wiley & Sons.

(For those interested in the relationship of the theories and principles of cognitive psychology to user-interface design. Discusses topics such as mental models, models of memory, skill acquisition and the psychology of language.)

Green, P. (1987). Human factors in computer systems: Some useful readings. _SIGCHI Bulletin, 19,_ 15-20.

(Describes a course in human factors and computer systems. A list of seventy course readings with full bibliographic information is included. Some of the topics covered include: displays, input devices, methods, models and editing, menus, windows, naming, filing, screen format, programming, furniture, and health.)

Hutchins, E. L, J.D. Hollan, & D.A. Norman. (1985). Direct manipulation interfaces. _Human-Computer Interaction, 1,_ 311-338.

(This article gives an overview of the characteristics of direct manipulation interfaces and speculates about some of the associated cognitive phenomena.)

Monk, A. (Ed.) (1985). _Fundamentals of Human-Computer Interaction._ New York, NY: Academic Press.

(Includes a series of introductory-level readings on topics such as input devices, displays, dialogue design, office automation and speech and expert systems. Also includes selections on experimental methods and statistics for behavioral research on user-interface issues.)

Mynatt, B.T. (in press). An Introduction to Software Engineering with Student-Project Guidance: Prentice-Hall.

(This text is designed specifically for undergraduate software engineering courses which are structured around student-team projects. Includes a complete chapter on user-interface design. User interface design precedes the chapter on preliminary design.)

Shneiderman, B. (1987). Designing the User Interface: Strategies for Effective Human-Computer Interaction. Reading, MA: Addison-Wesley Publishing Company.

(Like Shneiderman's earlier book, this book is an attempt to merge theoretical concepts and practical concerns. He focuses on an overview of some aspects cognitive theory early in the book. Issues of interaction style, interaction devices, evaluation, and social impact are discussed.)

Shneiderman, B. (1980). Software Psychology: Human Factors in Computer and Information Systems. Cambridge, MA: Winthrop Publishers, Inc.

(This book was an early attempt to merge concepts of human-computer interaction research and pragmatic concerns. As such, the first three chapters provide a basic description of a psychological model and an overview of research methods. Then topics such as programming style, software quality, team organizations, database issues, natural language, and interactive interface issues are discussed. The final chapter provides guidelines for the design of interactive systems.)

Sime, M.E., & M.J. Coombs, Editors (1983). Designing for Human-Computer Communication. New York: Academic Press.

(This book contains a series of articles about several phases of human-computer interface design. The first seven chapters focus to a large extent on general principles. The remaining five chapters describe particular interfaces. Not introductory reading.)

Smith, S.L., & J.N. Mosier. (1984). A Design Evaluation Checklist for User-System Interface Software. (NTIS AD A158 599). Bedford, MA: The MITRE Corporation.

(Provides a series of very specific guidelines - in the form of checklists for user interface features such as data entry, data display, sequence control, user guidance, data transmission and data protection.)

Ada Edu Project

Supporting the Use of Ada in Introductory Computer Science

Ravinder Chandhok
Terry A. Gill

Computer Science Department
Carnegie Mellon University
Pittsburgh, PA 15213

Abstract

The Ada programming language was designed to inherently support advanced software engineering. Thus, Ada is more than a language to the educator - Ada provides a framework in which to teach software engineering and computer science in ways not previously possible. However, most of the current emphasis in Ada development is involved with tools for the experienced programmer. These environments are usually too complex and bulky to be presented to novices in an early computer science course (based on the ACM CS1 curriculum). In addition, they usually require hardware that is too expensive to provide for large numbers of students. Therefore, in this paper we discuss a plan to construct an Ada environment for novices based on the *MacGNOME* environments already developed at Carnegie Mellon and being used on the Apple Macintosh. Through cooperation between the Software Engineering Institute, the Computer Science Department, Apple Computer, and Incremental Systems, Inc., we hope to put together a complete package including curricula, software (including support libraries), and a textbook to be used in teaching with Ada at the introductory level.

This material is based in part upon work supported by the National Science Foundation under grant number MDR-8652015. Any opinions, findings, conclusions, or recommendations expressed in this publication are those of the authors and do not necessarily reflect the views of the Foundation.

Introduction

The development of the Ada programming language has been heralded by many as the best language available to support concepts of modern software engineering such as data encapsulation and information hiding, strong typing and separate compilation. Due to the complex syntax and semantics required to express these ideas, Ada's impact in education has been limited to the more advanced courses. Introducing Ada at a late point in the curriculum can lessen its impact on shaping the behavior of the student, as many bad habits are already well established by this point. The lack of a well-defined Ada based curriculum and the obvious shortage of Ada instructional support materials have both contributed to the slow adoption of Ada at the introductory level.

In addition, most Ada compilers run on expensive workstations or mainframe computers. Although there are now Ada systems for the personal computer, they often require large amounts of memory that is expensive to add. These expensive machines are neither an option for teaching a CS1 level course which may have thousands of students a semester, nor are they an option for the smaller universities, colleges, and high schools across the country.

Despite the current situation, we maintain that a uniform Ada curriculum starting at the CS1 level can improve the quality of computer science and software engineering education. Since the current startup costs of moving to Ada based instruction are quite high in both manpower and money, we believe that if Ada is ever going to be accepted at the CS1 level then a programming environment and a curriculum must be constructed with the following features:

Novice Oriented

Any system to be developed must be targeted specifically towards the novice user. This may mean hiding or restricting some of the advanced features of the language to avoid confusion and unnecessary complexity. Advanced features within the environment such as data visualization and intelligent tutoring are necessary for guiding the novice through new material.

Language Support

The programming environment should eliminate the focus on syntactic details and maximize semantic feedback in all phases of program construction. In effect, the environment will *facilitate and support* a new language and curriculum by allowing the teacher (and the student) to concentrate on the computer science concepts instead of an idiosyncratic system.

Appropriate Textbook

In contrast to current CS1 books, an Ada textbook should take advantage of the richness of Ada to bring forth software engineering techniques early in the course. Moreover, the textbook must carefully expose relevant portions of Ada in a manner that defers mention of currently inappropriate features or details of the language. Indeed, direct translations of existing CS1 textbooks would be a mistake.

Novel Curriculum

The curriculum should enhance the material of CS1 by exploring new paths through the material not possible when limited by other programming languages. To facilitate this, a series of lab exercises coupled with larger programming assignments will be developed together with a robust software library. This incremental, hands-on experience has proven invaluable in the current CS1 course at Carnegie Mellon.

Therefore, in this paper we discuss a plan to construct an Ada environment for novices based on the *MacGNOME* environments already developed at Carnegie Mellon and implemented for the Apple Macintosh. Through cooperation between the Software Engineering Institute, the Computer Science Department, Apple Computer, and Incremental Systems, Inc., we hope to put together an educational package consisting of an integrated programming environment, instructional materials and the appropriate software support libraries.

An Ada Programming Environment for the Novice

The initial programming environment will be modeled after the current MacGNOME Project's Pascal environment (and all figures shown are from that existing environment). This environment has domain (or language) independent tools that support programming activities in addition to the standard language specific tools. Specifically, the MacGNOME environments (or GENIEs) are based on a structure editor. All tools communicate via this internal structured database, and thus the GENIEs are seamless in their appearance to the user. As shown in Figure 1, at any point the editor can inform the user of all possible syntactic constructions.

GENIEs also allow the user to edit any piece of structure as text, which is then added to the structured database via a parser. The combination of these two features allows the novice initially to construct their program via a menu, and then, as they develop expertise a textual (and sometimes easier) mode of construction can be used. The net benefit is that the teacher does not have to waste precious time on teaching syntax, but can instead concentrate on higher level concepts.

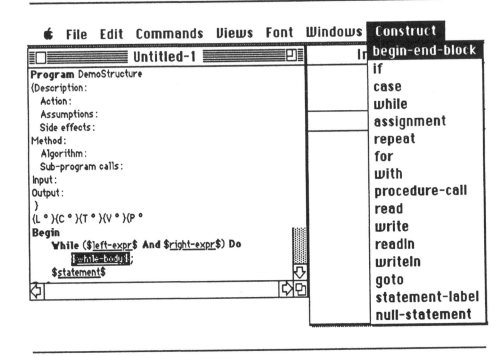

Figure 1 : Constructing a Pascal Statement

GENIEs also have the capability to provide multiple views of the structure database. These views can be used for editing, or just browsing. For example, th Pascal GENIE allows users to construct their program in a normal view, or in high level outline view which hides all executable statements. Also, the outlin view can be used as an index into the main view, which is extremely useful a programming assignments get larger. Figure 2 illustrates a Pascal program an its associated outline view. It is also important to note that all the views suppo structural editing operations - so you could first "rough in" the structure of you program in the outline view, and then fill in the details later in the main view.

Any number of views can be specified by the GENIE environment implemento and in an Ada environment one might imagine many specialized views tha would further aid in stressing the concepts of software engineering. F example, a documentation view which would only show the high level commen and structures in a package interface could be used in a library browser. Also, view that just shows the scoping of all the names in a package might be usefu The early parts of the Ada Edu project will concentrate on determinir pedagogically appropriate views to add to the environment.

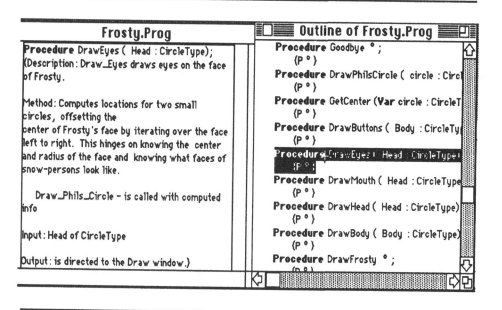

Figure 2 : A Program View and Its Outline

All the GENIE features mentioned thus far are concerned with providing a powerful system for program specification and construction. However, it is equally important to support a coherent model during the compilation, execution, and debugging phases of software development. In a GENIE, the compiler, runtime system, and debugger all communicate to the user via the editor. By virtue of this "lingua franca" for the tools, the GENIE implementor can easily add new tools to the system without forcing the user to understand a new command language. For example, breakpoints are set in the Pascal GENIE by pointing at the code and selecting "Set Mark". The run time system shows the program counter as a highlighted structure, which allows execution tracing to be more fine grained than the statement level. All in all, this allows for new and innovative forms of interaction with the user.

Advanced Features

Thus far, we have concentrated on the description of an environment to support standard operations like editing and compiling. However, to have a more substantial impact these GENIEs must integrate advanced features into the system that exploit the technology. These include a system for graphical display of data structures (including user defined types), an electronic textbook, and an efficient intelligent tutoring system. While these system components are generally not implemented in a domain independent fashion, the MacGNOME project has in its charter generic implementations of tools to support these features.

Data Visualization

In a novice environment, standard debugging tools that merely show ASCII representations of the program data are not sufficient. Novices are often taught about structured and dynamic data through pictorial illustrations but then build their programs in environments that force another view of the data upon the user. To avoid this confusing part of teaching, we feel it is essential to provide data visualization tools in novice environments.

The displays generated by the GENIEs will be generated to match the kinds of illustrations that the teacher would draw to represent the data structures. Figure 3a shows an example of how a record might be displayed. And as the GENIE provides a standard interface for programming tools, one might envision shaping the data display by manipulating the actual declaration of the type. Pedagogically, this could further enforce the notion that types are templates for data. In Figure 3b, a field in the record type declaration has been collapsed by the user (the field "center" is now displayed as "..."), a standard editing operation in a GENIE. Note that the resulting data display has changed accordingly. Again, due to the nature of MacGNOME environments, the data visualization piece of the system could be coupled to the runtime system to generate graphical views of the stack during execution.

```
Type
    namedCircle = Record
        name   : String;
        center : Point;
        radius : Integer;
    End;
```

aNamedCircle		
Name	'BigCircle'	
Center	X	10
	Y	5
Radius	5	

```
Type
    namedCircle = Record
        name   : String;
        ...
        radius : Integer;
    End;
```

aNamedCircle	
Name	'BigCircle'
Radius	5

Figure 3a: Data Visualization   **Figure 3b: Modified Display**

Electronic Textbook

Another important piece of the GENIE will be a facility to deliver course material and lessons online. The GENIE will do more than a simple display of a textbook in electronic form, it will have the capability of providing instruction on a module by module basis. A standard use of the electronic book would be to provide prose on a new concept, and then automatically execute the appropriate example. In this fashion a student might move through material in a more self paced fashion.

Above and beyond the implementation issues of an electronic book tool are the problems of having the appropriate material to deliver. Textbooks meant for cover to cover reading often are confusing when sections are presented out of order (as could happen in the electronic form). The success of this part of the system depends heavily on having appropriate modules in a form suitable for online delivery. The Ada portions of this material will be developed as part of the Ada Edu project.

Intelligent Tutoring

In and of itself, the electronic book provides useful remedial help and reference for the user who understands what to study next. But often the novice is at a loss to identify his or her current conceptual roadblock. By adding an intelligent tutoring system to the GENIE, we can guide the student's progress in the fashion of intelligent computer aided instruction (ICAI).

Traditionally, CAI systems have been rigid in their interactions with the student. Work is underway as part of the MacGNOME project to build a domain independent tutoring system that allows for flexible modes of interaction with the student. For example, the teacher can indicate to the tutoring engine when to report errors and warnings and can also choose between enforcing temporal ordering or allowing a more relaxed problem solving behavior.

The structure of the tutoring system is beyond the scope of this paper, but what is important to note is that the interface between the tutor and the rest of the world is the GENIE itself. Therefore, upon observing a certain kind of error the tutor might call up the electronic book to provide a remedial lesson, or the tutor may disable the ability to execute a program until the design satisfies the teacher's specifications.

Many different kinds of tutoring interaction will be researched during the development of the tutor and the appropriate lesson base for Ada. It is unclear at this point in time what the final system will provide, but it is evident that the leverage from the other parts of the GENIE will aid in the development of an effective tutoring system.

Instructional Materials

As mentioned before, the success of the Ada Edu project depends also on the development of appropriate instructional materials. Unfortunately, it seems to be easier to specify the programming environment than it is to spell out what comprises the correct instructional material. The next part of the paper explains the concerns and overall goals of our curriculum development, but does not attempt to fully qualify our directions.

Curriculum Design/Introductory Textbook

The curriculum development component embodies the 'what' and the 'how' of delivering an Ada-based introductory level course. The 'what' has been widely researched by professional organizations and their recommendations for a CS1 course have been published. On the other hand, the 'how' is a wide open issue and we feel that our programming environment, support libraries, and instructional materials will allow us to design a unique CS1 course. That takes care of the 'what' and the 'how' for CS1 but a more interesting set of questions is 'what' parts of Ada are appropriate and sufficient for a CS1 course and 'how' are these pieces best taught? The project hopes to address both questions. The instructional materials will include, but not be limited to, lab modules, programming assignments, sample case study programs and packages, lecture notes, tests, and, of course, a set of mastery examinations. In conjunction with the curricular development, an introductory CS1 textbook will be written that emphasizes modern software engineering techniques. The focus of the textbook will be in developing program 'architects' rather than 'carpenters' by providing a rich base of components from which to start. Although the instructional support materials and the CS1 textbook will be tightly coupled to the resulting programming environment, the majority of the materials will remain generic enough to allow for adaptability throughout the educational community.

Instructional Software

The instructional software materials that are developed will facilitate the delivery of the course by providing a rich library of reusable routines. The extensive collection of packages will make it possible for CS1 students to glue together complete Ada programs early thus making it possible to focus on software engineering issues throughout the course. This approach of building programs from existing routines encourages a disciplined development approach. The students will be introduced very early on to the necessary engineering principles of abstraction, information hiding, modularity, and certainly top-down design with the unit of focus being the package. As they become more familiar with Ada and its implied methodology, the students will begin to create their own packages, which will necessitate a much closer look at the details of the language and eventually the students will be contributing new components to the libraries. Consequently, the students will have exposure to both programming-in-the-large and programming-in-the-small. Indeed, the development of sample programs, case studies, and smaller routines for purposes of student analysis, modification or direct use will also be a significant part of the software component.

Time Line

The plans for this project include a structured integration into the curriculum at Carnegie Mellon, with the following approximate schedule. The project will begin in April 1988. The first user-interface design and a vanilla structure editor will be ready by October 1988 when the compiler integration will start. A working system will be available by September 1989. The first pass at a curriculum and a sample of the software packages will be completed by September 1988. At this time all the materials generated will be made available for critique by interested parties.

The proposed textbook will be started during the summer 1988 and be in draft form by Summer of 1989. This draft will be used during the Fall 1989 in a test class at CMU.. Also by the Fall 1989, the software libraries and instructional materials will be near completion. The programming environment will have data visualizations, a simplified form of the intelligent tutoring system, and a help system ready for the initial classroom testing during the Fall 1989. The instructional materials, software libraries, and the environment will go through final modifications and refinement while being used in selected courses at CMU during the 1989-90 academic year. It is hoped that all introductory computer science courses at CMU will adopt the Ada based curriculum by the Fall 1990.

Conclusion

It is well known that the adoption of Ada at the undergraduate level has been deferred because of the lack of appropriate instructional materials, textbook support, and a suitable programming environment for the beginner. The Ada Edu Project plans to help in all three areas. In particular, the programming environment will not only make the teaching of Ada much easier but it will make the teaching of Ada a very attractive alternative. The development of reusable software packages as the backbone of the course will facilitate the early introduction of software engineering methods and provide the means to extend the CS1 course far beyond the traditional programming course.

General References

1. Chandhok, R., et al. "Programming environments based on structure editing: The GNOME approach." *Proceedings of the National Computer Conference* (NCC'85), AFIP, 1985.

2. Garlan, D.B. and P.L. Miller. "GNOME: An Introductory Programming Environment Based on a Family of Structure Editors. *Proceedings of the Software Engineering Symposium on Practical Software Development Environments.* ACM-SIGSOFT/SIGPLAN, April 1984.

3. Garlan, D.B. "The VIZ Unparse Specification Language and the VAL Unparser." Technical Report, Carnegie Mellon University Computer Science Department, June 1985.